Unfinished
Love Story

CAROL B. BOST

xulon
PRESS

Copyright © 2016 by Carol B. Bost

Unfinished Love Story
by Carol B. Bost

Printed in the United States of America.

ISBN 9781498470476

All rights reserved solely by the author. The author guarantees all contents are original and do not infringe upon the legal rights of any other person or work. No part of this book may be reproduced in any form without the permission of the author. The views expressed in this book are not necessarily those of the publisher.

Unless otherwise indicated, Scripture quotations taken from the Holy Bible, New International Version (NIV). Copyright © 1973, 1978, 1984, 2011 by Biblica, Inc.™. Used by permission. All rights reserved.

www.xulonpress.com

Contents

Chapter One:	Enter Salvador	7
Chapter Two:	I'll Keep You	11
Chapter Three:	School Days	15
Chapter Four:	Holidays Hurt	17
Chapter Five:	Welcome Back!	21
Chapter Six:	Chosen	24
Chapter Seven:	Permission Granted	28
Chapter Eight:	Miracle at the Mall	33
Chapter Nine:	Cinderella Night	41
Chapter Ten:	Stroke of Midnight	49
Chapter Eleven:	Fishing Fun	53
Chapter Twelve:	Tough Love	59
Chapter Thirteen:	Love Note	63
Chapter Fourteen:	Clean Treasures	67
Chapter Fifteen:	Say the Words	69
Chapter Sixteen:	Summer Surprise	73
Chapter Seventeen:	Real Mom	76
Chapter Eighteen:	And Love Remains	78

Chapter One:

Enter Salvador

"I hate you, and I will make you hate me too!" Those were such harsh words coming from an eight-year-old boy. It seemed impossible for one so young to be filled with anger and hatred toward a complete stranger. What had I done? What had I said? I had only known this youngster for about two hours. After all, I was a teacher, filled with love and a desire to educate and mold young lives. How could these venomous words be hurled at me in such a short time?

This wonderful and true love story all began in October of 1987 when the school secretary knocked on my second-grade classroom door with a small, unkempt, undesirable student who was to be assigned to my classroom of twelve underachieving readers.

"Good morning, Mrs. Bost. I have a new student for you today," said Mrs. Mason, the school secretary. "His name is Salvador Garcia, and he has recently moved into our area."

"Good morning, Salvador, it is good to meet you," I responded kindly. She handed me a manila folder, offered a quick smile, and walked back down the hall to return to her duties in the school office.

"Welcome, Salvador; let's find a seat for you, and introduce you to all your new classmates." As a teacher of very active and curious second-graders, I didn't lose a minute finding a seat for the "new boy" and playing our favorite introduction song by Hap Palmer, "What Is Your Name?" This song offered a chance for the children to sing out their names in keeping with the fun tune. I knew it would be a warm welcome and an interactive way to introduce our new friend to our small family. So far, so good! The children always enjoy getting a new student in the classroom and were quick to open arms of love to the "new boy."

As we finished the introductions and were certain that Salvador felt at home, I returned to the small reading groups, while the students worked with the assistant teacher, Mrs. Wilmarth, on their seatwork. The morning schedule had been interrupted, but the students were so glad to have a new friend and to miss some of the traditional morning seatwork, so all was well; or at least I thought it was.

In the reading circle at the back of the room, I continued meeting with groups of five to six students who had been placed in this special classroom because of reading challenges or lapses in their developmental growth in the language arts. The state had offered this individualized instruction with a full-time aide to assist these children. We had such a nice world with lots of love and specialized assistance in reading. Little did I know at this point that our little family's dynamics was on the brink of being turned topsy-turvy.

Not long after our classroom had returned to its normal schedule and I was enjoying the small reading group at the back of the room, I was interrupted by the screams and pleas for help from the sweetest little girl in the room—Candy. Her name certainly fit her disposition. She was a hard-working, kind, and pleasant student who always showed love to others. I couldn't imagine what had happened.

"Candy, Candy, what in the world is the matter? Why are you crying?" I queried.

"The new boy just hit me in the back, and it hurts," she cried. "I really don't know what I did to make him so mad." After checking her back and calming her down, I asked my assistant, Mrs. Wilmarth, to take charge of the class while I called the new boy outside to further investigate this incident.

"Salvador, did you hit Candy in the back? If so, why did you do such a thing to her? We do not have these outbursts in my classroom, and I do not tolerate such behavior." As I bent down to be eyeball to eyeball with this angry young student, I was further shocked to hear the response from one so young and new to our school.

"She made fun of my name, and I hate her!" came the furious reply. "And I hate *you*, and I will make you hate me too!" Never before in my eight years of teaching had I been met with so much opposition from a student. I knew something was terribly wrong.

"I am not sure why you hate me, but I love you; however, I cannot allow you to take your anger out on the other boys and girls in the classroom," I sternly responded. "Our classroom operates on friendliness and respect; therefore, this behavior cannot continue. " This rebuke only fueled more bursts of fury and harsh words from our new boy.

"I hate you; I hate this school, and I hate *everybody*! I will make you hate me too."

Knowing that "a soft answer turns away wrath," I gained my composure, and said again to Salvador: "Salvador, I don't care how much you hate me; I am here to help you, and I love you. Nothing can make me hate you. You are a very special young man, and I know that you have much ability inside of you. I know that you are very smart, and I want to help you. I will love you, and nothing can stop that love. You may choose to hate me, but I will choose to love you."

At that moment in time, I did not realize to what degree those words would be tested in the days and months ahead, but I thought I was ready to begin this journey, and I knew that it would be unlike any I had traveled before.

That first school day with Salvador finally ended, and not soon enough for me. After the students had all filed outside in the hallway to wait for the buses, I settled down with that manila folder that had been handed to me earlier by Mrs. Mason, the secretary. What information did this hold for me that I really needed to know? Who was this young, hurting student who had been quickly placed in my care? What had happened in his short eight years that had made him so bitter toward the world? As I began searching the papers inside, all those questions were answered. Some of the answers shocked me, and others informed me that Salvador had been mistakenly placed in my classroom. According to the documents, he was a very gifted reader and had high potential. My students had reading impairments and were here for the individualized assistance. This was a major mix-up! He didn't belong with me.

This child had behavior issues, not academic ones! He had been abandoned by his birth mother as an infant, been placed in numerous foster homes who could not continue handling his outbursts of anger, and now was living in a boys' home not too far from our elementary school campus.

Why did the office personnel and administrators think they could just place him in the smallest classroom in the school and be done with it? At first, I felt violated, that I was just being used to make room for this troubled child. It was not fair, and I knew that I could not allow this situation to steal an otherwise positive environment for the others. I had to inform the principal that a terrible mistake had been made, and that Salvador needed to be placed with one of the other eleven second-grade teachers, not me. Dealing with his anger and negative behavior was not what I wanted for the other students, who, by this time in the school year, were making positive strides toward filling in their academic gaps. I realized that I had a very strong argument for his removal, with the paperwork to prove it.

Since the long day had ended, and all the students were gone for the day, I marched straight to the principal's office to state my case.

"Good afternoon, Mrs. Mason. May I please speak with Mr. Cain?" By the tone of my voice and the urgency in my step, Mrs. Mason knew that I meant business.

"I am sorry, Mrs. Bost, but he has gone to a very important meeting, and will not be available until in the morning. Is there anything I can help you with?"

"Yes, there is." I replied. "The new boy that was assigned to me earlier today certainly does not belong with *my* second-graders. I read his background information, and he is an average reader; my class is designed for the lower level readers. It became very obvious as the day progressed that he needs another placement. His behavior issues are simply despicable, and I refuse to allow his challenges to stop the progress with my students. He needs to be removed immediately," I vented.

"Mrs. Bost, Mrs. Bost, surely we can discuss this with Mr. Cain when he returns. I will make a note of this, and make certain that he sees you first thing in the morning."

Realizing that nothing could be done for the moment, I thanked her, and trudged back to my classroom, carrying a heavy load from a very disheartening day. How could I continue like this if nothing could be done? I felt sure that Salvador Garcia needed much more than I felt I was capable of giving. Again, I was very mistaken about that. The plan for this young man was far greater than I could even begin to imagine.

Chapter Two:

I'll Keep You

Wednesdays are very busy days for youth pastors, and since my husband and I were serving in this capacity, I needed to get home and prepare for the evening ahead. Those high school students that I taught during the midweek service were full of energy and enjoyed the lessons we provided for them; however, on my short drive home, I realized that my energy level was in the negative range. How could I teach any more on this day? I was empty. Salvador had really drained me.

It didn't take but one glance at me for my husband to ask the dreaded question: "What happened to you today? You look totally worn out." It was then that I walked him through the events of that fateful day, and with a heart full of sympathy and love, he responded, "Stay here tonight, Sweetheart. I will take the youth classes for this evening. You really need some rest."

He didn't have to beg me to remain at home for some rest. I had just lived through the toughest day of my teaching career, and I wanted some quiet time. It was during this quiet time at home that I knew I had to be silent and seek God for some answers. As I lay on the floor, totally exhausted, I cried out to God for help and direction. Was this really a mistake? Was there a divine purpose that was too big to realize at the time? Why had Mr. Cain not been available to me? It seemed that I was left all alone to face this struggle within myself, yet I understood that I did not have the answer. As I remained quiet and still, reflective about the day's events, God began to whisper to my heart: *"There is no mistake; you are the one to teach Salvador the meaning of real love. Keep him, and I will show you what to do with him. There is a much bigger purpose than what you can see right now. Don't worry about how you will do it, or what will happen to the other children. This is* my *plan, and it will not fail. Your responsibility is to obey and follow Me."*

Those really were not the words that I had hoped to hear, but I knew that this was an ordeal that was way over my head, and I needed the divine guidance from my Heavenly Father to move forward. It was when I gave up my will, and allowed God's presence to cover my weariness that I felt an unexplainable peace flood my entire being. I was supposed to keep Salvador. This really was *not* a mistake.

Picking myself up from the carpet, I now had a resolve and inner strength that was burning inside me—a deep desire to keep this undesirable student who had given me the most challenging day thus far in my young career. Now, I was equipped; I was ready, and I knew I could not quit. What a stark contrast from only about ten hours earlier that day.

Thursday morning dawned, and with it came a crisp newness in the day. It almost felt like the first day of school for me, even though it was a beautiful fall morning in October. I was full of anticipation as I drove the fifteen miles from my home in Tyler, Texas to the elementary school in Whitehouse, Texas where I taught. Those second graders always made me feel so special and loved each day; I really loved my job. My heart was pounding like a new bride as I approached the building, wondering how Salvador would feel about me on this second day of our acquaintance. I was certain that I had a new perspective on our relationship, and that it was right for him to be placed with me, regardless of what the paperwork had stated.

The morning began without incident, but it wasn't long until Mr. Cain heard the report from the school secretary that one of his second grade teachers had had a very upsetting day the day before. Being the kind and strong leader that he was, Mr. Cain's voice could soon be heard outside my classroom door. My assistant, Mrs. Wilmarth, answered the door and summoned me immediately.

"G—g—ood morning, Mrs. Bost," came Mr. Cain's booming, but nervous voice. I could tell by his facial expression and posture that he dreaded this conversation, as if he knew something that I did not know. "I heard that you needed to see me yesterday, and I apologize for not being available. That is why I wanted to see you first thing this morning. I understand that you had quite a difficult day yesterday, and I certainly hope we can work something out for this new kid. He is one like we haven't seen around here. I am not sure I know what to do with him. I just felt that you would be the right one for him. He needs so much more than the academics; he is just a very challenging case."

"I know, Mr. Cain. It didn't take long for our world to be turned upside down yesterday, and I did *not* want to keep him in this room. He had temper tantrums, spoke harshly and disrespectfully to me, and simply did not cooperate on any level. That is the reason I came to speak with you. When I read the report concerning his own academic ability, I *knew* he did not belong in this setting, and I thought there must have been a huge mistake. I came to see you, with the request that he be placed in a classroom with other students of his ability. I did not want his actions and behavior to deter this group of students from meeting the goals and objectives that we have placed before them. It seemed so unfair to me yesterday, but today, I have a different perspective. After much prayer and quiet time with my Heavenly Father, I now agree with you. I am supposed to keep Salvador, no matter what the records declare. He was meant to be placed in my classroom, with these students, for the remainder of this school year. I will give this my best effort, not allowing him to disrupt, while at the same time, focusing on the needs and goals of the twelve other students that I have. We can do this! I assure you that I will give it my best, and with Mrs. Wilmarth's patience and loving assistance, this year will continue to be successful."

"Oh, thank you, Mrs. Bost; I just knew when I read his report, that your classroom was the perfect place for him. Thank you for being so flexible and willing to tackle this huge project. There is not another classroom that I feel would fit Salvador. His needs far outweigh the ones that can be met with books, paper, and pencils. You will do fine with him, I am sure. Again, I appreciate your willingness to help. Remember, we are here if you need us."

With those words of confidence and affirmation, Mr. Cain turned and headed back to his office, to give the "good news" to Mrs. Mason. I am sure they both felt at ease, knowing they would not have to deal with that same angry teacher that had appeared in the office just one day earlier.

With all the "official" business taken care of, I was now ready to begin day two with my "new boy." What a tremendous challenge lay ahead of me, what new territories to be explored, and today, I felt excited, happy, and eager to have this young man in my class.

Chapter Three:

School Days

As the students entered the classroom on that morning, I greeted them all with a heartfelt "Good morning" and a warm smile. Salvador's face displayed indifference and a coldness that I cringed to see. It brought back vivid reminders of the day before, but I leaned on the strong resolve and positive decision to keep this young man and make a difference forever in his life. More than that, I was confident that God had led me to this path for this season, for this time.

The second week with Salvador continued with little difference; we worked, and Salvador lived to get outside so he could run, jump, and mostly play soccer with his new-found friend, Wiley. Most of the work that we did was not new to Salvador, and as I listened to him read, the facts from the curriculum folder were confirmed: Salvador Garcia was a very good reader and a very capable student of second grade work. In fact, he may have been *above* grade level in some areas. The only problem was that his interests lay only in playing, and not in showing his academic prowess. As I encouraged him to do is work, conflict arose. Salvador reminded me often that he hated me, and that he would make me hate him too. Those were difficult times, and often, I questioned the decision I had made, allowing him to remain in my classroom. But I knew that I must stay the course, and remain focused, even more so when those questioning thoughts arose. Many times my mind would travel back to that Wednesday evening when I wrestled with the idea of keeping this little boy, and I could vividly recall the moment when God gave me the peace I needed. He also had equipped me for this task. He never asks anything of us that He won't empower us to complete. I had to allow those words to comfort me again and again: *"There is no mistake; you are the one to teach Salvador the meaning of true love."*

So many times in our journey, Salvador lacked the necessary school supplies to be successful, so I recall buying pencils, crayons, notebooks, paper—just about anything that he needed. When he became upset with me, he would throw the supplies on the floor, and scream, "I don't want your old pencils; I hate you!" I certainly felt like throwing them back at him in a similar response of: "OK, I won't buy you anymore, and I don't love you either." But I knew that this was *not* what God had in mind when He chose *me* to be Salvador's teacher. I had to make a difference, and to *be* love to him. After all, that is one quality that this eight year old had never experienced, and my mission was to teach him. What an incredible assignment. There are so many times in life when we cannot do what is required of us—at least, not with our own natural abilities. It is during times such as these that we absolutely *must* "lean *not* on our own understanding."

October raced by, with only fewchanges on Salvador's part. He continued to show disrespect and anger toward me and his classmates. I daily asked God for the love to pour out on him. Many times, mine had been exhausted. He really enjoyed playing soccer with his friend, Wiley, so often I would be forced to take away his play time so he would at least do *some* of the work that he was so capable of doing. This surely made him dislike me even more, but I also knew that real love had to be tough, so I wearily made him accountable and tried my best to do what I said I would do regarding his discipline and correction. These were difficult days, but I stayed on course, counting the days until Thanksgiving and then Christmas breaks. I really did need time to rest and refuel, and I thought that Salvador would need a break from *me*, too. I am sure that in his little mind, this could not be love.

Chapter Four:

Holidays Hurt

Holidays are such wonderful times for adults and children as well—times to focus on family, love, and the importance of traditions. Thanksgiving finally arrived, but with it, came my own curiosity of how Salvador would spend this very family-oriented holiday. As my husband and I spent time with our friends, my thoughts would wander back to that cold orphanage, where a little eight-year-old boy lived among older teens and uncaring adult supervisors. What would he eat? Who would be around to say grace and give thanks? How did he feel? What was going through his young mind? I had only wished things could be different; we wanted to share love with this precious little boy and receive love back from him. At this point in time, that was only an elusive dream. Thanksgiving weekend came and went, and before we knew it, we were back into the school scene. Young students are very excitable during holiday seasons and naturally more difficult to control, even under the best of circumstances, and so the holiday season brought more struggles, anger, outbursts, and the daily battle of the wills. Salvador was convinced that he could control me and that he would, in fact, *make* me hate him. With God's help, I displayed that tough love and structure that I was sure he needed on a daily basis. It took prayer, and a daily dose of God's Word to make it through those turbulent times.

"Love is patient, love is kind. It does not envy, it does not boast, it is not proud. It is not rude, it is not self-seeking, it is not easily angered, and it keeps no record of wrongs. Love does not delight in evil, but rejoices with the truth. It always protects, always trusts, always hopes, always perseveres. Love never fails." (I Cor. 13:4–5a). This passage certainly was one of the many that brought hope to me as I sought refuge and direction going into the month of December.

I knew that Salvador would not have much to look forward to during the Christmas break, and it was my heart's desire to make Christmas special for him. Since my husband's family and my family lived back in North Carolina, we already had plans to go there for our holiday, as usual. "Just what would happen if we took Salvador with us?" I thought. "What if we purchased a plane ticket for him and allowed him to have a *real* Christmas? Oh no, that wouldn't work; we already had our reservations; it was probably too late anyway." Thoughts such as these bombarded my mind as the day for Christmas break drew closer and closer. Finally, one day at dinner, I reluctantly brought the idea to my husband.

"Honey, what do you think about taking Salvador to North Carolina with us for Christmas? I just can't stand the thought of his spending another holiday in that bleak, cold orphanage. We would simply need to purchase a plane ticket for him, and let our families know that we are bringing a special boy home with us. I am sure everyone would enjoy the delight and excitement of an eight-year-old boy at Christmas! It would be nice, don't you think?"

"Sweetheart, that does sound easy, but you know we will have to gain permission from the home, and probably even from the state of Texas. Have you given that much thought? I do like the idea, but let's be realistic here. There is so much more that we would have to do. Certainly, you haven't spoken of this to Salvador, have you?"

"Oh no, I really didn't want to say anything too early; I wouldn't want to disappoint him! He has had enough of those in his young life. If you are agreeable, I will make a call to the director of the home tomorrow and see what we have to do to make this happen. I am getting excited just thinking about it."

With no opposition from my husband, and excitement burning inside me, I went to sleep that night, dreaming of sharing the perfect Christmas holiday with a little boy who had no idea of what a holiday filled with real love was all about. Imaginations of good food, lots of toys, attention from a family who would simply adore him, and teachings of the true meaning of Christmas were all good reasons to anticipate such a holiday break. I just knew that I could convince the authorities at the home that this was the right thing to do. I was sure of that.

The next day at school was very normal, with the students making colorful Christmas decorations and talking excitedly of the upcoming holiday. Salvador was relatively quiet when it came to this topic, knowing that he did not have much to look forward to. My heart was torn and sad when I heard expectant giggles and excited conversations about trips to Grandma's house, and vacation plans for the break. I really wanted to let Salvador in on the secret, but I knew not to speak before I had all the information. Self-control had to be practiced on days like these.

Almost at the sound of the last bell, I made a hurried escape to the office to make that highly anticipated phone call. Once I had the approval, I could break the news to Salvador, and we could begin making our detailed plans. I could not wait.

Pulling the phone number from the pocket of my blazer, I dialed the number for the orphanage. With sweaty palms, and a racing heart, I waited! "Please answer, someone. I have an important request to make." Soon, a strong male voice could be heard on the other end.

"Good afternoon, you have reached East Texas Home for Boys. How may I help you?"

"Hello, this is Carol Bost, Salvador Garcia's teacher from Whitehouse Elementary. Could I please speak with the director?"

"He is on another call at the moment; I will be happy to assist you."

"Yes," came my nervous reply. "I would like to inquire about the possibility of taking Salvador home to North Carolina with me and my husband for the Christmas holiday. Is this something you can help me with?"

"Ma'am, I am not sure you understand the magnitude of your request. This boy is a ward of the state of Texas and is not allowed out of the state for any reason. He will remain here with the other boys and enjoy a fine holiday that we will prepare for them."

At that moment, my heart sank. I had really thought this would be possible. I just knew that this trip was a part of God's plan for me and Salvador. It would be the perfect way to show true love at the most special time of the year.

I further implored, "Please, sir, we will take full responsibility for him. Just allow us to do this. Our intentions are good; we are fine people. We only want what would benefit this kid. We will take care of him."

"Mrs. Bost, I certainly appreciate your holiday spirit and desire for good will, but the law is the law, and we don't have the authority here to break it. I am so very sorry. Salvador may not leave the state of Texas."

With those disheartening words, I thanked him, and placed the phone back in its cradle.

Christmas break: two full weeks away from the classroom and the usual rigorous schedule. This should be a happy time for any teacher, but for me, the holidays seemed heavy. My thoughts strayed to the image of a little boy, who would be sleeping in a top bunk on a hard mattress with an orphanage full of older boys who also were angry and hurting. How could that possibly be Christmas for him? Where were the smiling faces? Where was the anticipation of awaking on Christmas morning to the smells of breakfast cooking, Christmas lights, and toys under the tree? Would he even hear the story of the Baby Jesus? What about visiting Grandma and Grandpa's house to show off the new games? These questions and more plagued my thoughts as the day approached to say goodbye to the students.

Finally, it came—the last day of school before Christmas break. On that long-awaited December day in Whitehouse, Texas, I bid each of my students farewell for the holidays, and sadly wished Salvador a "Merry Christmas." I was so glad that I had not shared my dream of taking him with us; I certainly did not want any more disappointments in his life. As the students filed out the door, parents greeted their youngsters with excitement and anticipation of the treasured time together! My heart melted as I waited with Salvador to catch the bus to the orphanage.

"Bye, Salvador," I said. "I will see you in a couple of weeks."

Returning to my room, to pack up my things, I could not stop the tears from falling. I was glad the students were gone, as I needed time to collect my thoughts and to try to find some answers to the million questions still zooming around in my head. This was Christmas break. Cheer up. Get ready to go home to North Carolina to celebrate with family. This is life. Get a grip. I could do this.

When the desks were finally straightened and the last paper tossed in the waste basket, I made my way to the parking lot to begin my own Christmas vacation. I knew I could not allow this sad plight to affect such a wonderful season of the year for my husband and family. They were very excited about the season and it really would not be fair for me to dampen their spirits.

Chapter Five:

Welcome Back!

Christmas vacation came and went and with it, haunting thoughts of the little boy who had no one, the little boy who hated me and who would make me hate him too. But, I didn't hate him. I was concerned for him, and I could not stop the waves of compassion and care that swept through my mind on a regular basis. I did enjoy the season with my family and husband in North Carolina, but oddly enough, I was ready to return to the classroom in January just to see this little boy who hated me and who would make me hate him, too.

That first day back in January was a quiet one, the students ready to return to some sense of normal schedules and routines. Salvador did not have much to say. It seemed he was lost in another world, another dimension. When the students drew pictures of their favorite toy received or their favorite food eaten, he simply scribbled and mumbled under his breath. I surmised that his holiday probably wasn't a pleasant one. Later that afternoon, I announced that the next day would be "show and tell."

"Boys and girls, tomorrow you may bring something special to share with us. It may be a toy or a game that you really like and would not mind sharing. You may have a few minutes to show us what you have and tell why it is so special to you." Salvador seemed to like this idea, so I was encouraged. I was sure he had received some toys and candy from area charities and community groups. Surely, he would enjoy sharing with us.

The next morning brought happy faces, and delighted squeals from the students who had, indeed, brought special gifts they had been given.

Of course, Salvador came in empty-handed and angry. Even though he said he did not care that he had nothing to share, I knew he felt otherwise. As William, Candy, and Lewis shared their toys, Salvador simply stared through them. When the students had finally finished sharing their treasures, we prepared for our afternoon art lesson. This was sure to bring a smile to Salvador's face and allow him the chance to be involved. I quickly arranged the tables and chairs for the activity and prepared the supply table with crayons, chalks, paints, and lots of paper and glue. This was a time for the students to express their creative abilities and show off the artistic talents that so many displayed. I was glad that "show and tell" time was over, giving this little boy a chance to escape the pain that he must have been feeling deep inside.

It wasn't long into the art activity that I heard a distressed scream coming from across the room.

"Mrs. Bost, Mrs. Bost, please stop Salvador!" came a panicky cry from Lewis. As I turned quickly to see what had alarmed Lewis, I noticed that Salvador had made his way to the cubbies, where the children stored their book bags, coats, and lunch boxes. This, of course, was where I had asked them to return the toys they had brought to show.

Startled and upset by what I saw, I immediately made my way to the cubbies to take Lewis's truck away from Salvador. He had bent the front fender of the truck, and upon seeing me heading toward him, proceeded to stomp the truck and totally destroy what had meant so much to young Lewis. As I looked more closely, I observed that other toys and games were certainly not in the same condition they were earlier in the morning! Salvador, in his own moments of jealousy and anger, had taken his frustrations out on the students who had brought the toys. What a mess.

It is true: "Those who are hardest to love need it the most." What a wise, honest, yet challenging statement. Salvador simply could not stand the fact that what he longed for the most seemed impossible for him. The jealousy and anger inside of him had erupted, and he wanted to make the others feel as he felt.

"Hurt people hurt people." While I was familiar with many of the proverbs and famous quotes from others who had dealt with adversity, I still wanted to go back and retract my decision to accept this troubled young man into my classroom. He always seemed to create chaos out of whatever good thing we attempted to accomplish as a class. I also knew that it was too late now, and that I must stand strong on the decision that I had made. Certainly, something good was going to come of this.

"Salvador, Salvador, you will not be allowed to play outside this afternoon," I promised. "There are no excuses for this type of behavior. You must apologize to Lewis, Amanda, and Brandon, *and* you will write a letter to their parents." At a loss for what to do next, I consoled the distraught students and placed the broken toys in the appropriate book bags. Dealing with the parents would not be pleasant either.

During the Christmas holiday, I had hoped that things would be different when we returned for the second half of the school year. I guess I was wrong about that. It was a mistake to think that just time away from a situation would make it all better. They say that "absence makes the heart grow fonder," and I had really missed Salvador, but, again, not much had changed with his behavior.

As we continued into the cold days of winter, Salvador soon realized that he must complete his daily work in order to play outdoors with his good friend, Wiley. This was a good thing and made my life easier, to some extent. Salvador was coordinated, quick on his feet, and very athletic. This made him an excellent soccer player and popular with the students when it was time to go outside for recess. It was encouraging to see a very healthy relationship develop between him and Wiley. They lived to hear me say, "Boys and girls, it is time to line up for recess." I, in turn, enjoyed watching them interact and burn off that energy that had been pent up inside all morning. It was times like these when I saw smiles, laughter, and joy coming from this injured and wounded boy. It was a very beautiful thing to see, yet I wanted to do more; I wanted to give him the family that he desired and needed. Just maybe something wonderful could still come from this otherwise negative situation. I was certainly not one to give up easily.

Chapter Six:

Chosen

As we all worked our way through the last few weeks of winter, our focus turned to the upcoming spring weather, more outside activities, and yes, the annual spring music festival. This big event occurred in early May, and all of the kindergarten, first, and second grade students looked forward to singing and dancing for the parents and community. This was quite an eventful night in Whitehouse, Texas, and to be involved in this program was surely an accomplishment. I was anticipating a great program, and 100 percent participation from my special class of talented second-graders. Yes, I even had big dreams for Salvador as well. What would our class be without him? Even with the struggles, and difficult days, the other boys and girls had come to realize that he was a part of our family now too. The fun days on the playground, and the excitement he showed during music class only helped the other students realize they had much in common with this new kid. He really had found a home among us.

Now, with the spring music festival just around the corner, the students especially looked forward to the Tuesday and Thursday afternoon visits to see Mrs. Andrews, the music teacher. It was during this time that she encouraged them to sing and dance to the best of their abilities, as only the best singers and dancers would be given the main parts in the big performance. It was a desire of each second grader to be selected for these roles, since the second graders were the oldest students in the school and loved the fun and attention this night always brought. All this was new to Salvador because he had not attended our school in the earlier years. It seemed that Salvador enjoyed the music class, as he was usually the first to line up. I wasn't sure if he just liked the class, or if he was happy to get a reprieve from the afternoon work that I required of him. Whatever the case, both he and I welcomed these classes on Tuesdays and Thursdays. Every elementary teacher looked forward to the special classes such as music, physical education, or foreign language because it offered a chance to take a small break and prepare for the next lesson, and I was certainly no different.

I will never forget that Tuesday afternoon when I stood at the door of the music room, waiting to pick up my energetic and excited second graders. Mrs. Andrews was running a little late, so I patiently waited for her dismissal, so I could take my students back to the classroom for math time. When they finally formed a line and came out to the hallway, I could feel the extra life and energy that was pouring from them. There was an unusual excitement and even a little sneaky attitude that was different, but very evident. What had happened in that music room? Somehow, I felt that it was good, but it generated some questions from me.

When we entered the room, the students did not go immediately to their seats as usual. They formed a line at my desk, yelling, jumping, and asking questions.

"Mrs. Bost, Mrs. Bost, guess who has the main part in the Spring Music Festival?" they asked. "Guess who can dance better than anyone else?"

"Can you believe it? Can you believe it? Guess! Guess!"

"Boys and girls, please, settle down. Give me a chance to hear you! One at a time, please. Candy, can you tell me what is going on?"

"Mrs. Bost, can you guess who has the main part of the dancer in the spring music program?"

"OK, let me see . . . is it Wiley?" I knew that Wiley had great coordination, and that he was quick on his feet when playing soccer.

"*No*," came the quick response; "guess again."

"How about Brian?"

Again, with arms waving and faces smiling, the unwavering answer was, "*No!*"

Searching each face with an inquisitive glance, I spotted Salvador at the back of the group, smiling sheepishly, as if he was hiding something. I could tell he wanted to say something, but he was watching me intently to anticipate my next guess.

By this time, the energy and excitement in the room was explosive, so I knew I had to make one more very important guess. Since second graders are not good at keeping secrets, and since all eyes had bounced back and forth to Salvador, I was certain that he was the lucky one.

"OK, I will make one more guess; is it Salvador?"

"*Yes, yes*, responded twelve ecstatic students, while one special student grinned and acted a little embarrassed by all the commotion. I was certain this little boy had experienced a first-time rush of emotions as he finally knew what it felt like to be wanted, needed, and—yes, chosen. I could barely hold back my own excitement and joy at the thought of his showing skill and coordination before the entire school and the small community.

After spending some time in settling the class down, I knew we had to get back to business and do our math lesson for the day. With a million ideas racing through my head, I did manage to complete the task and keep the students settled. It seemed that all we could think about was the great opportunity that had just been afforded one of our very own. We were all proud of him and could not wait to see just how he would react. After all, wasn't this the same young boy who *hated* me and wanted me to hate him too? Wasn't he the one who had angrily pounded little Candy on the back that first day he came to our school? I guess we all had the same questions: Would this be successful? Had Mrs. Andrews made the correct selection? Only time would answer these and other questions.

The days leading to the music festival were busy indeed. It remained difficult to keep Salvador's attention on academic subjects because he was constantly watching the clock to see if it was time for music class. Since we only went to music class on Tuesdays and Thursdays, I took this as an opportunity to encourage Salvador to do his work well so he could practice his dance when it was time for the class. In many ways, this helped. Never before in his young life had he been given a goal to reach, a promise to keep, or an opportunity to prove anything to anybody. He certainly did not think he had a talent, and now, he had been selected, chosen, picked. What a different world for this second grade boy.

Thursday afternoon's music class could not come quickly enough for me. The students' energy was contagious, and I could not wait to peek into the music classroom to see this talented Salvador in action. It certainly would be unusual to see him excited, involved, and productive in any setting. This always brings joy to a teacher's heart, and I was overdue to experience this for myself with this young lad. After lunch that day, all eyes watched the clock for the long-awaited music time. Of course, Salvador was the first to remind me that Mrs. Andrew's would be waiting, and that we should *not* be late.

"Boys and girls, it is time to line up for music class now," I eagerly announced to the class. Of course, Salvador was the first in line and no one wanted to argue with him about who would lead the line. The other boys and girls seemed to *want* him to go first and were happy to have the lead dancer in their class. The dynamics in this little family was positive, and I was proud of the way the students had offered him support and love, in spite of his previous rebellious and negative behavior. It is amazing how forgiving, accepting, and loving young children can be, even in adverse situations.

Those music classes became more intense as the time for the program drew closer, and Salvador's anticipation of the special night increased as well. During this time, I was convinced that I had done the right thing in agreeing to keep him in my class. It was indeed a happy time. I was proud of the little guy, and I just knew he would not disappoint me, his classmates, or the school community. Sadness still crept in when I considered the fact that he would not have a proud mom or dad there to cheer him on as he displayed his talent on that big night. It would hurt to see other parents there with cameras poised and faces aglow, watching their young performers bring joy to the audience. How would Salvador react to this? Would he become angry and ruin the show? My mind drifted back to the other times in class when jealousy and anger changed how Salvador responded. Hopefully, it would not happen *this* time.

Chapter Seven:

Permission Granted

Finally, the long-awaited day arrived: the Spring Music Festival. The entire school atmosphere was charged with energy and excitement. Every year, the Spring Music Festival spelled not only fun but the approaching end of the school year. It was each teacher's challenge to keep her classroom focused and complete the day's schedule without too much interruption. After all, this was the evening that brought the entire community together to celebrate young talent and dramatic ability. Parents smiled, and teachers swelled with pride as they watched precious little ones sing, dance, and perform as if they were on Broadway. And to think we had the main actor in our little classroom family. I knew that I must work hard to keep their attention on this special Tuesday.

The day began without incident, and before we realized it, the time to prepare for lunch arrived. As students were washing their hands and putting away materials, I felt a slight tug on my skirt. Turning around, I noticed Salvador, an inquisitive look on his face. It seemed he wanted to say something, but didn't know quite what to say. I had come to understand much of his body language by this time in the year.

"Well, Salvador, are you excited about tonight? It's almost time. I'm sure you will do a great job."

"Yes, came his quiet reply. "I'm ready. Are you going to be there, Mrs. Bost?"

"Why, of course, Salvador; I wouldn't miss this event for anything in the world. My plan is to get my work done here so I can be back for this special night."

It was at this moment when I again realized that my little performer had something really important on his mind. Sometimes it was hard for him to share his feelings with me, but I patiently waited. After a short awkward silence, the words finally poured out.

"Mrs. Bost, do you think I can wear what I have on today? Does it look OK to wear for the program?" came his muffled and embarrassing questions.

At these words, my heart sank. The worn jeans, the discolored shirt, and the small dirty tennis shoes he had on would *not* work for the big night, but how could I tell him?

"Oh, Salvador, I responded, what about those darker jeans you have with that striped shirt? That outfit really looks nice on you. Why don't you wear it tonight?" I hesitantly asked, trying hard to mask the pain I felt inside. I was sure that all the other performers would show up in nice new outfits, walking beside proud parents and grandparents toting cameras and bouquets of flowers. And now, reality again hit me, as I realized that this young man would experience none of this on his big night. I really did not know what to say, as I searched for the right words. The look on his little face said, "What should I do next?" And I was the only one he could ask for help. It was certain that the male counselors at the home had not taken the time and energy to establish rapport with him, much less to be concerned about what he wore.

"This will have to work," came a quiet and sad response. "That outfit you just mentioned is in the dirty clothes bin; my washing night is on Wednesdays, and I can't get the clothes out of the dirty bin. Our clothes are only washed on the night when it is our turn."

"We'll talk about this after lunch, Salvador," I responded. "It's time for lunch, and we can't be late."

All of a sudden, my hunger and excitement for lunch disappeared, and in its place came an intense desire to find a way to help this struggling boy.

"Mrs. Wilmarth, please take over; I have a very important errand to run in the school office." Again, I was thankful to have a full-time aide to assist me, allowing me the opportunity to manage challenging situations such as this one.

As I watched my students enter the lunchroom doors, I quickly made my way to the main office to begin a process that I prayed would yield the positive results I so desperately wanted.

"Please, Lord, I prayed, give me the favor I need today to make something wonderful happen for this little boy who really needs a miracle."

Reaching for the phone on the cradle, and the phone number for the orphanage, I began to dial the number to East Texas Boys Home. With my heart racing, and a million questions zooming through my head, I began to see a fairy tale night for me and Salvador.

"Hello, this is Carol Bost, Salvador's teacher at Whitehouse Elementary. May I speak to the director, please?"

"One moment," came the friendly reply.

I could see it now. I would take Salvador to the mall, get him some new clothes, stop by a favorite fast-food restaurant to pick up some dinner, and then meet my husband at home for a family-style evening before we headed off to the school to watch this top performer dance to his heart's content. He *would* have a family tonight; he *would* be made to feel special, and he would look good doing so.

As I waited for the director, my heart raced, my mind envisioning the plan. "Just allow me to take him," was my earnest plea. "Lord, You told me to keep this boy; now please come to my rescue and make a way for this request to be granted. I trust You, and I really need Your help like never before."

Soon, the same male voice that I recognized before Christmas could be heard on the other end.

"Good afternoon, may I help you?"

"Yes, sir; this is Carol Bost, from Whitehouse Elementary, Salvador Garcia's teacher. How are you this afternoon?"

"I'm, Mrs. Bost; how may I assist you today?"

"Well, Mr. Greely, I first want to make sure that you are aware of the special Spring Music Festival that is to be held at the school this evening. I am certain Salvador has mentioned it to you."

"He did say something about that, but we can never guarantee any special favors once the boys get home from school each day. So much depends on the behavior that they exhibit once they get off the bus. Evenings can sometimes be very hectic around this place, you know."

"Yes, I can imagine they are very difficult, especially with so many different age groups and all the homework assignments. Your job there is a tough one, I am sure. Well, the purpose of my call is to make sure Salvador is able to come back tonight, and to ask a very special favor of you. You see, he was selected to be the main dancer in tonight's performance, and we surely would not want him to miss the event. The whole performance revolves around his dance on center stage. He was selected from all the second-grade students, and our class is very proud of him. He is one talented little boy with lots of energy and ability. I do not want him to miss this big night."

"Oh, Mrs. Bost, I can hear the excitement in your voice, but I cannot make any promises about his attendance this evening. We have to make sure homework is done, dinner is served, all medications are administered, and all chores completed. This is usually not done without arguments and distractions. We will give it our best effort, but that is about all we can do."

"Mr. Greely, what are my chances of taking Salvador with me after school? I would promise to do all the above-mentioned tasks as well as purchase some new clothes for him to wear tonight. My husband and I would take care of his dinner, get him ready, take him to the program, and then return him back to you at the proper time. I strongly believe that this opportunity may just be what Salvador needs to boost his self-esteem and set him up for success the rest of the school year. He seems to be very positive about being chosen, and he really wants to do this. I am not sure if the program will be successful without him. Is there any way that I can sign him out for an evening?"

"This is another difficult request, Mrs. Bost, but if you will hold for just a minute, I will speak with his housing supervisor to see what he thinks. We need to come to an agreement regarding this. No one has desired to do such a thing before. Hold on; I will be back in a few moments."

I really did not think "moments" could last so long. As I stood in the school office with the phone in my hand, I could see out into the large cafeteria where the students were having lunch. Salvador was eating and laughing with his friends and probably looking forward to his once-in-a-lifetime performance, slated to begin in a few more hours. I was his only lifeline, his only hope for a fairy-tale evening.

"Please, Lord make a way for this to happen. Help those in authority at the home see beyond the dirty face, the torn clothes, and the disrespectful attitude. Help them to see a broken boy who only wants to be loved. Help them say 'yes'" to my request to take him home for the evening. What a memorable night for him. What a memorable night for *me*. Lord, I only want to help; I am only obeying You. Now, do what I cannot do. Make the impossible *possible*."

After what had seemed like an eternity, a male voice could be heard on the other end jolting me back to reality. "Hello, Mrs. Bost. Thanks for holding. I did get to speak with Salvador's housing supervisor, and together we have made a decision. I really do not know why I am doing this, but as the director of the home, I am going to allow you to take him for this evening; however, you must understand that he is property of the state of Texas. You must be fully responsible for anything that could happen to him during the time he is in your care. There are several documents that have to be signed, and you must also agree to feed him and administer his evening medications. In addition, he will have to be returned to our premises by 9:00 PM and no later. Do you think you can take responsibility for all this? Is this still something that you want to do?"

"Yes, of course, Mr. Greely, I have thought long and hard about this, and I will take full responsibility for him. How do we proceed?"

"I will have my assistant bring the documents and his medication to the school this afternoon before dismissal. You will have to sign all the papers, releasing us from any possible law suit or danger. You must understand, Mrs. Bost, that he will be under your total jurisdiction, and that if anything happens to him you could possibly be sued by the state of Texas. This is quite an undertaking; however, if you still are certain of this, I will have the papers to you before you dismiss the students for the day. I can somehow sense how important this is to you, and it is my sincere hope that it will help this troubled young man."

"I cannot thank you enough, Mr. Greely, and yes, I take this very seriously, and I will do whatever is required of me to get Salvador. This is a very special night for him, and for me! I will be expecting your assistant; just check in at the school office and someone will direct you to my classroom. Again, I appreciate your willingness to make this happen. I promise to have him back to the home before 9:00 PM tonight. Thank you again."

With that final "thank you," I rushed to the cafeteria to help my assistant get the students lined up for their afternoon activities. It would be quite a challenge to keep this quiet until the last bell of the school day, but I knew I could do it.

Chapter Eight:

Miracle at the Mall

What a busy and loud afternoon we had. The students could barely sit in their seats and do their math lesson for the day. All thoughts and minds had already been tuned into the evening's program and the wonderment of what it was going to be with the "bad kid" on center stage for most of the night. Even though the students were proud of Salvador, the idea of his being perfect and respectful was more than they could imagine. I guess I had the same questions myself, but hope was strong inside of me, and I *knew* this night was going to be unlike any we had ever experienced.

As the afternoon dragged on, I found it difficult to keep my eyes from moving to the small glass panel in the classroom door, watching, waiting for the workers from the home to bring the papers for me to sign. Even though I was given permission to take Salvador at the day's end, there was still an element of doubt in my mind. Was this really going to happen? Where were they? I could feel the tick-tock of each heartbeat, keeping time with the steady beating of the clock. This was anticipation as I had never experienced before.

Earlier, I had given the good news to my assistant, Mrs. Wilmarth, so that she could keep the students' focus on their centers so I could discreetly answer the door and speak with the representatives from the home when they arrived. I was careful not to tell Salvador, as I wanted to spare him any unnecessary disappointment should this plan be foiled. This young man certainly had had enough pain and disappointment in his young life, and he did not need any more.

Finally, with the day almost to a close, my eyes caught a glimpse of an unfamiliar form outside the classroom door. They were here at last. Now, I could take a deep breath and relax. Quietly and carefully, I made my way to the door to take care of this important business. This was really happening.

"Hello, Mrs. Bost; my name is Luke Montgomery, one of the counselors at the boys' home. I have been told to deliver these documents to you and return the signed forms to the office. I am sure you have been expecting me. Did Mr. Greely explain all the details to you?"

"Good afternoon, Mr. Montgomery; yes, I have been waiting for you. I am so glad to meet you, and I thank you for coming this afternoon. I am prepared to do whatever is necessary to take Salvador for the evening. I have been told about his medications, his dinner, the required time for his return, and the seriousness of this venture. Is there anything else I need to know?"

"It sounds as if you and Mr. Greely have it all worked out. I just want to warn you, Mrs. Bost. This kid can be very difficult to manage. He often lashes out at us, hits other boys at the home for no reason, and has no remorse when corrected. He is a bundle of trouble, and I cannot imagine how he may act in the presence of other adults he may not be accustomed to. Are you really sure this is something you want to tackle?

"Oh, Mr. Montgomery, this is something I have prayed for. Yes, I am up for the challenge. I sincerely believe that Salvador will perform at a high level tonight, and I do think I am doing the right thing for this youngster. Now, what forms do I need to sign?"

Sensing the confidence and certainty that I displayed, Luke fumbled through his brown leather briefcase to retrieve the forms and the small bag of medication that he had brought from the home's office. Luke was hoping that I would be tense and back out. I know he was uneasy about my taking on this seemingly fruitless project. But the vision and dream within me only burned brighter. I was sure this was going to be a success.

With a slightly shaking hand and a racing heart, I signed my name on every form. There was a form that said I must administer his medication with his evening meal. There was a form that said I had to have him back by 9:00 PM sharp, and there was a form that released the home from any possible problem during the time he was in my care. In other words, any challenge or problem was totally my responsibility. With all events happening so smoothly, I was never more certain that this was going to be just fine.

"OK, OK, I thought. Just let me get this all done so I can go and tell the good news. No, wait. I must stay quiet until after the final bell rings, and the last student leaves for the day. I must not create a more hectic ending to this very busy and chaotic day. I will have to wait until the students line up for their buses and only Salvador is left. But, how will I do that?"

"Mrs. Bost, Mrs. Bost, do you have any questions before I leave?" The final questions from Luke quickly interrupted my harried thoughts.

'Oh, no, Mr. Montgomery, I think everything has been made very clear to me. Again, I thank you for being so cooperative and helpful. I promise to take good care of Salvador, and to have him back at the home *before* the 9:00 PM deadline. I appreciate your assistance and advice. This will be a very eventful night for both me and Salvador."

"Yes, I am sure "eventful" is a good way to put it. Good luck, Mrs. Bost. I certainly hope things turn out well for you and Salvador tonight."

With that encouraging word, Luke Montgomery turned and headed for the double doors at the end of the hallway, leaving me holding the small medication bag and tons of questions. Still, the anticipation and dream for the night could not be relinquished. This was going to be a successful and memorable night. I just knew it, and nothing or no one could change that—not even Salvador himself.

Now, the next step was to make sure I handled every detail to perfection. The hands on the classroom clock seemed to weigh a thousand pounds each as the remainder of the afternoon slowly dragged on. Finally, it was time to pack up and prepare the students for dismissal. All those who were bus riders had to line up in the hallway and wait for their bus number to be called. I made sure that students had their belongings, and with a smile and a hug, I bid each one good-bye. This was my daily ritual. Each boy and girl in my classroom knew they were loved. As usual, Salvador was the last in line.

"Bye, Mrs. Bost; I will see you tonight," came the excited response from Candy. "I can't wait for the program."

"See you in a little while," exclaimed Brian. "You are going to be surprised when you see our dances."

Unfinished Love Story

"I am sure you all will make me a happy and proud teacher tonight. Now hurry along; the time will be here before we know it."

Salvador slowly moved toward the door, making his way to his usual spot in the hallway to wait for bus 615.

"Are you sure you are going to be here tonight, Mrs. Bost?" he sheepishly asked.

"Yes, certainly, Salvador, but I have a question for you before you leave. Would you like to go with me to get dinner, shop for a new outfit, and get ready for the big show?"

"*What*? Yes, I would, but you know they would never let me do that! I need to hurry, Mrs. Bost; my bus will be leaving soon."

"Wait, Salvador, do you really want to go with me?"

"Mrs. Bost, I do need to hurry and catch my bus. I hope someone will bring me back tonight. I really want to do this, you know; I have to go!"

"If you really want to go with me, Salvador, I will take you."

"But I will only get into more trouble if I don't get off that bus at the home this afternoon. I want to be good so they will let me come back tonight."

I then pulled the small medication bag and paperwork from the jacket pocket on my vest. "Look, Salvador, everything has already been arranged. I have *permission* to take you. . . . *if* you want to go. Mr. Luke came by the school earlier and dropped off your medicine for this evening. I called and asked if you could come home with me, and they said 'Yes!' Can you believe it?"

"*Really?* I can't believe that they would let me go with you. I never get to do anything special. What do we need to do now? I will be able to come and dance tonight for sure, won't I?

Salvador's excitement at this point was contagious. He began to jump up and down, expressing emotions that I had never seen from him. All the trouble I had gone through up to this point was worth it, just to see his happiness. It was my guess that this moment was probably one of the happiest of his short life, except for the day Mrs. Andrews gave him the news that he would be the main dancer in this Spring Music Festival. The smile on his little face was worth more than the lunch I had sacrificed to arrange this.

"Let's hurry, Mrs. Bost. I'll wash the boardI'll pick up all the paper on the floor."

Immediately, this "troubled" second-grader turned into a perfect little teacher's helper. He smiled and chatted endlessly about how messy these kids were, and how he could not believe they would leave the desks in such disorder. As he hurried around the room, cleaning, I simply marveled at the positive change he had so quickly displayed.

As the last desk was straightened, and papers placed in my briefcase, we were now ready to embark on our fun and eventful evening. It seemed that Salvador was truly in another world.

"Come quickly, Salvador," I said. "We have a few stops to make, and we must hurry to get back to the school in time."

"OK," came his obedient and respectful response. "May I carry your briefcase for you?"

Just who was this child? I wondered. The change that had come over him was remarkable.

For a moment in time, it seemed that one happy teacher and one small excited second-grader had a common mission—a plan to succeed, a plan to do what had seemed almost impossible only a few days ago.

Walking excitedly to the parking lot, I realized that we were making a memory that we would not soon forget.

"Which car is yours, Mrs. Bost?" asked Salvador as we exited the building and stepped out onto the small paved parking lot.

"Over there," I said, "the orange sports car with the black top." At that time I drove the coolest car of all the teachers at Whitehouse Elementary School—a 1982 burnt orange Audi Fox stick shift.

The look on his face at that point said it all. What a contrast from the ugly orphanage vans that he usually was seen in.

"Hop in, Salvador; we must hurry to the mall and get a nice outfit for you. That program will be starting before we know it, and we cannot be late. I don't want to keep the star performer from his stage tonight," I chuckled.

"Can I change the gears?" Salvador asked as we approached the highway leading from the small school to the city.

"Yes, just be careful, and ease the stick into the next position. This is a four-speed, and when we get into the last gear, you will be able to hear the smooth sound of the engine." I proceeded to explain to Salvador just how a stick shift works. He had a blast, leaning on every word. He took it all in, changing gears, pretending to be a stock car driver. This was a fun and memorable time for both of us.

"Hey, Salvador, what kind of outfit do you think you want for tonight? Remember . . . you are the main dancer; you will be on center stage all by yourself for a portion of the program. You must look good.

"Well, I really want a pair of those stone-washed jeans that everybody is wearing. I have never had any of those, and I think they are the best. Wiley has a pair. Do you know which ones I am talking about?"

"Oh yes, I know, Salvador." At this point, my mind began racing about budgets, prices, and costs. I knew that I only had a certain amount of money to spend for an entire outfit, and these jeans alone would take most of the amount I had in mind. I had wanted to get everything that he needed to make this night perfect—pants, shirt, shoes, and socks. I did not want to disappoint him, but I knew that I only had a small amount of money to spend, and it was my desire to stretch it out, allowing enough to purchase all the necessary items.

"Stone-washed jeans are nice, Salvador, but if we get those, I will not be able to get the other items. They are very expensive, you know. Would you rather just have the jeans, or would you like to choose another type of jeans that do not cost as much, and get a new shirt, and shoes to match?"

It did not take long for Salvador to realize that the whole outfit was the better choice. I already knew that he was a smart young man, and giving him a choice in the matter was the right thing to do.

"Oh, I would prefer the whole outfit. I do need a new shirt and some shoes—some good tennis shoes that would be good for dancing and moving on the stage. I will take that choice. Are we almost there?"

"Yes, right around this next corner, and we will be at the mall. Just remember that we do not have lots of time to spend; we still have to pick up some dinner, go home and eat, and then get dressed for the festival. I am so excited that I can hardly wait. Are you getting nervous?"

"I am not nervous at all; I just want to see all the clothes in this store and try on some cool jeans. "

The thought of taking an eight year old shopping—who had probably never been in a mall before—caused a little anxiety on my part, not to mention that I had no experience shopping for a child, other than picking up a birthday present for a niece or nephew. This was truly going to be an interesting experience, to say the least. Luke Montgomery's words rang in my ears: "I am sure 'eventful' is a good way to put it." What had I gotten myself into? I was not even sure what size to begin looking for, and I was certain Salvador did not know.

Wheeling into the first empty parking spot I could see, I took a quick glance at my little performer. He had such a look of anticipation and happiness on his cute face. I wondered what was going through his mind.

"Here we are, Salvador. Let's go into this side door and make a stop at the department store. I am sure they will have just what we are looking for."

We hurriedly found the children's department, grabbed a shopping cart, and began our adventure. Salvador was quick to locate the boys' jeans, and almost ran to where the tables lay full of all colors, styles, and sizes of boys' jeans and pants.

"Here, Mrs. Bost, here they are. Look at all these jeans and pants for boys. I just love these."

Salvador began picking up one pair and then another, smiling and commenting about how he just loved each one.

"OK, let's find a few pairs that you *really* like, and we can take those to the dressing room. I am not sure what size you wear; do you know?

"Oh, look, I am sure these will fit."

This was truly a special time in this young boy's life—a shopping experience with a teacher who was not sure herself just what to do.

Eyeing each pair for length and waist size, I could only make a guess at what size we should take to the dressing room.

I finally allowed Salvador to pick five pairs that he really liked, hoping that we would be successful in getting one good pair to fit properly.

As he ran off to the fitting room, I remained in the boys department, just waiting to give my opinion about each pair. It wasn't long before a shrill, "Mrs. Bost, Mrs. Bost, these look great; I love them!" could be heard throughout the entire store, or so it seemed. As I exchanged puzzled looks from the shoppers around me, I replied to Salvador: "Please come out so I can see."

I know it must have been a funny sight—one small Hispanic boy and his light-skinned "parent" attempting to find just one pair of jeans that would look nice and fit appropriately.

As Salvador emerged from the fitting room area, I immediately had to hide my laughter. The jeans he had selected were at least two inches too long with enough room in the waist to fit the both of us. It was a funny sight, and I am sure those around the store thought the same thing.

"I love these, Mrs. Bost; they are just perfect. Can I get these?"

"Well, Salvador, I really think that pair is a little long, don't you think? And we do want to find a pair that will not fall off as you are on stage dancing. Let me check the size so I can get a different size for you."

After a few trial and error attempts in the dressing room and unusual glances and stares from fellow shoppers, we found a very nice pair of pants, a cute shirt, and even socks and dancing shoes for the star performer. To complete the outfit, we added a pair of suspenders to give it a real "Texas" look.

With everything we needed for the night, Salvador and I quickly made our way to the mall exit. I am quite certain this was the first time this young man held in his hands packages containing brand new clothes that he had picked out himself. The spring in his step and the grin on his face was both priceless. Now, we had just a short time to pick up a quick dinner, meet my husband to eat, and get ready for the magic to begin.

Chapter Nine:

Cinderella Night

"What would you like to eat, Salvador?" I asked, as we drove away from the mall. "We only have a couple of hours until we have to be back at school to line up for the grand entrance. We both have to be early. Remember, I have to get all the students in our class ready to join the other classes on the side of the stage. We cannot be late."

"Oh, Mrs. Bost, do you think I could get a Happy Meal from McDonalds? I have heard so much about them, and I am sure it would be good. You get a toy in there too, don't you?"

"Yes, you do, Salvador. There is a McDonald's on the way to our house, so we can easily pick up what we need and meet Tim at home."

My husband, Tim, worked at our church as youth pastor, and with his busy evenings, would not be able to attend the music festival with us. Even though we would miss him, I had already made plans to take plenty of pictures to capture this fun evening.

Driving to the pick-up window, I gave the order to the attendant, and chatted happily with my little friend. At this point, he almost seemed like a son to me. It seemed a perfect fit. I was a loving young teacher with no son of my own, and he was a special little boy with no mom or dad to call his own. I think we both were relishing these moments of what some would call normal family times.

Salvador helped me count the money to pay for the order, and we sped off. Salvador's one hand clutching his first ever Happy Meal, and the other hand on that stick shift! How could life ever get any better? I wondered if Salvador had ever dreamed of being "normal"? Had he ever hoped for a real family? What did he dream of and think about in his little world as he tried to drift off to sleep at night? For me, I had often thought of how I would spend time after school if Tim and I had had a little boy or girl to share life with. This was undoubtedly one of those moments when I would have liked time to stand still.

Driving up the to our modest, Texas-style rancher, I knew we did not have a minute to spare. Tim had already arrived from work, so Salvador and I grabbed the parcels and hurried inside to have dinner and get ready for show time.

"Hi, Honey, did you have a good day? Well, hello, this must be Salvador. I have heard so much about you. I am Mr. Tim. It is so good to meet you."

Tim extended his hand, and Salvador slowly shook his hand, uttering a quiet, but friendly "hello." I am sure these formal introductions were a bit different for my small friend. I could only imagine the many emotions he must have been experiencing at that moment.

"I really wish you could go with us tonight, Sweetheart," I said as I turned to my husband. "As you know, Salvador is the star dancer tonight, and we have the perfect outfit for him to wear. We found it at the mall a little while ago."

"Yeah," came Salvador's jubilant response. "Look at my new jeans, shirt, and shoes. I even have some of these suspenders." Clutching the treasured purchases, he proceeded to pull every item from the bag and show each one to Tim. If anything could break the ice and start a meaningful conversation, these clothes were sure to do it. This little guy had turned into a different person. It is always interesting to see how a little love and attention can give a person new eyes, providing a better view of himself. My heart was full of love and excitement, as I had been somewhat concerned about just how Salvador and Tim would respond to each other. This was almost perfect.

"Let's hurry and eat," said Tim; "I want to see you model this outfit before you both leave!"

"Thank You, Lord," I whispered as we sat down for our family dinner.

We each took our seats at the dining room table, and with bowed heads and grateful hearts, Tim gave thanks for our food, asking blessings upon Salvador's performance at the school. It was a picture-perfect moment: a young husband and wife, with a small and excited eight-year-old boy, experiencing for the first time what most children have the privilege of experiencing years earlier.

We ate quickly, chatting about school, Tim's work at the church, but most of all, focusing on this young dancer, who was in a new world of his own, and he seemed to love it. "This is good," Salvador said, as he munched on his burger and fries. "I am going to eat it all."

"You do that," I encouraged. "You will need all the energy you can get to perform those dances tonight. There will be a big crowd there, and all eyes will be on you. Are you ready for that?"

"Yes, I just hope I remember everything I am supposed to do."

"Oh, you will," Tim interjected. "Mrs. Bost has told me all about how hard you have worked and how awesome this night is going to be. Please do not forget to take pictures. Do you have enough film in the camera, Honey?"

"Yes, I checked on that a few days ago. I surely do not want to miss capturing this show. I will be right up front so I will be sure to catch this dancer in action."

It did not take long for Salvador to finish his meal. The next important thing to do was to take a shower and finally to dress in that crisp new outfit. There certainly was not a minute to waste.

As Tim and Salvador made their way to the guest room, I looked through my closet to find the perfect dress to match the colors in Salvador's outfit. That was not hard to do; I had a dress with the identical bluish-green color to match his slacks. Perfect! We would almost look like mother and son. I was feeling a bit nervous as I finished getting ready, but as Tim picked up the camera to take a few snapshots of us, I knew both Salvador and I were ready for this great night.

After saying our goodbyes and receiving Tim's well wishes, Salvador and I were off. It was about a seven-mile drive through the rural Texas countryside to the elementary school where I had been an elementary teacher for two years. Few words were spoken on our short ride as images of what was about to happen were dancing in our heads. This moment did seem like a dream, and I think we both were nervous, yet very happy about what was just on the horizon.

Finally, as we pulled into the teacher's parking lot, Salvador quickly burst from the car door, almost running to the side entrance to enter the building. He did use caution as he moved and turned his head; he did not want to mess up his hair or soil his perfectly new outfit. I chuckled under my breath. This was certainly not the usual behavior displayed by my little friend. It was encouraging to see how the time, love, and attention had made such a difference in his world. I smiled just to see Salvador in this light.

Dressed and ready

We made our way to the classroom, where many of the other second graders and their parents were waiting. There was a buzz of excitement and anticipation in the room. The next step was to arrange the singers, dancers, and other performers in the order that Mrs. Andrews had requested for the grand entrance on stage. Salvador was to enter at the back of the line, as he would approach the stage at the beginning of the performance. Under normal circumstances, Salvador did not like to be near the back of the line, and he was not afraid to hit and kick his way to the front. The other students simply understood his selfish ways, and in order to prevent a fight, they would allow him to push his way to his desired spot at the front of the line. But not tonight. Salvador wanted to avoid a fight at all costs. After all, he did not want to soil his new clothes and mess up his neat hairstyle. His walk to the back of the line was almost statue-like. I did manage a small giggle as I directed the other students to the hallway. Stage time had finally arrived.

With all the kindergarten, first, and second graders in place, Mrs. Andrews approached the stage with a smile and an excitement that was felt throughout the auditorium. This night was the highlight of the year, and this time, a new star was ready to make his debut. With camera in hand, and a racing heart, I scanned the faces until I saw him. There on the front row stood my Salvador. Our eyes caught for a second, and he waved. One red-haired kindergarten girl screamed, "Mom, where is Grandpa?" The audience burst into laughter, and then Mrs. Andrews announced the first act. Salvador took his place on center stage for the dance. All eyes were on this new kid that no one had recognized from the small tight-knit community. A parent next to me asked, "Who is that kid?" Proudly, I smiled and said, "He is with me." I watched as this unwanted, unloved, and otherwise problem child brought the audience to its feet. His footwork and coordination were unprecedented. The other singers and dancers took their cue from their leader. For just a small moment in time, I was the proud mother of a star on stage, and it felt good. I am sure my "son" was relishing this moment as well.

Finally, when the last song was sung and the final dance completed, Mrs. Andrews announced that all were invited to stay for refreshments in the cafeteria. Several hundred stars wanted to replay each moment over cookies and punch. My bright star ran to me for a hug and affirmation. "Can we stay for refreshments?" he asked. "Yes, for a little while, Salvador. Remember I have to have you back home by 9:00 PM. I do not want to be late. We may want to do this again, and I have to keep my promises."

As we made our way from the auditorium to the cafeteria, I felt as if I was escorting a celebrity. Every parent, teacher, and guest wanted to know just who this great dancer was. I smiled and proudly responded with, "He is a new student in my class this year, and he came with me tonight. Didn't he do a wonderful job?"

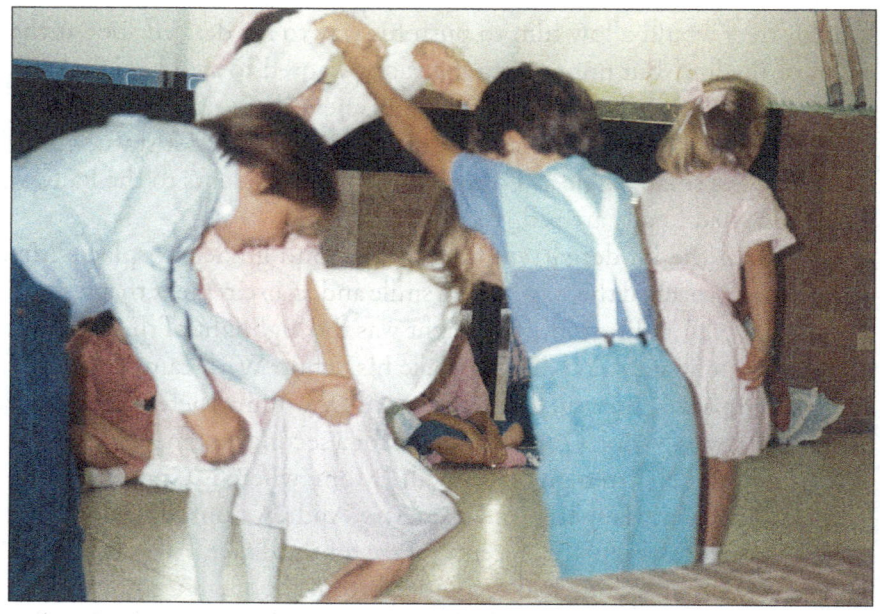

Dancing Fun

As we munched on cookies and posed for quick snapshots from parents and teachers, the time seemed to fly. Aware of the time, I mentioned to Salvador to finish his snacks as we had to head back home. Since this was our first true outing, I realized the importance of having him back at the proper time. I could still hear Luke's voice as he reminded me: "This kid can be very difficult to manage at times. Is this something you really want to do?" If only the boys and leaders at the home could see him now. This has been the perfect evening, I thought; I really did not want it to end.

"Come on, Salvador, we must be heading to the car. Tell everyone good-bye. You will see them all at school tomorrow. It is already 8:40, and we have to leave."

With cookie in hand, a grin of satisfaction on his face, and a poised look of success in his stride, we turned and moved toward the outer hallway that led to the parking lot. The fairy tale night had almost come to a close. The most difficult part of the entire day was about to begin, the drive home and the good-bye at the door of the orphanage. I could only guess how hard it would be for this eight-year-old, boy. It was not going to be easy for me. I whispered a prayer as we quietly walked to the parking lot. There, in the same place I had parked it a couple of hours ago, sat the cool orange Audi Fox that would take us to our dreaded destination. Only a few words were spoken as the tired performer climbed aboard and buckled his seatbelt. Why did all good things have to end? I wondered.

Salvador and classmates

Unfinished Love Story

A Night to Remember

Chapter Ten:

Stroke of Midnight

Driving along the quiet country road, I thought about the day and felt a ray of satisfaction in the midst of the struggle that was going on inside of me. I was glad it was dark in the car, as I did not want my little friend to see the uncertain look that I am sure was evident on my face. It was, indeed a quiet ride thus far.

After about two miles, my silent thoughts were interrupted as desperate and shocking words erupted from Salvador. "Don't you want to adopt me, Mrs. Bost? No one would care if you did. I could just go home and live with you and Mr. Bost. There is no one who would even miss me. I think I would like that. Could you?"

Totally astonished with his query, I fumbled for the right words to say in this delicate moment. "Why, of course, Salvador, I would love to adopt you, but it is a process, and would involve lots of time. I have to return you to the home tonight as I promised Mr. Greely and Luke. They expect to see you before 9:00 PM. Remember; I gave them my word that I would bring you back. We would have to speak with the proper people in authority as well. Besides that, what would everyone at the home do without you? You are so very important to them."

"No, I'm not," he responded. "There is no one who would care, and no one would even notice I was gone."

"What about your foster mom that you mentioned to me a while back? She would not know where to find you, and she would miss you."

"She would not care; believe me. I really would like to stay with you. Nobody needs me. I am always in the way, and I get into trouble, no matter how hard I try not to."

Again, I was thankful for the darkness in the car, as tears pooled in my eyes. I knew I could not allow him to see me cry. He was only yearning for this great evening to never end, as I was. This was becoming a little complicated at this point, so I drove on, hoping we could change the subject or just talk about the events of the evening. He seemed to be stuck on this topic, so I explained to him again that I had to keep my promise to the home, but we would be able to talk about it later.

As we neared the boys' home, I again told him how proud I was of him, and how much I had enjoyed the time together. I reminded him that we would see each other in school the next day.

"You can wear your new outfit tomorrow," I said. "It is not dirty at all. You only had it on for a few hours, and it really looks nice on you."

Turning into the driveway, I quickly brushed the tears from my eyes, and prepared to tell him good-bye when we approached the door. He was silent and very thoughtful. Only a few hours ago, this energetic second grader was full of life, changing the gears in my car, and chatting nervously about the performance. Now, all energy and life seemed to have dissipated. Oh, how I wished I could have fixed his situation.

It only took a few short knocks on the door to arouse a small army of young men from within. Salvador was the youngest of the boys in the home, and it seemed he had to fight for his very survival. The boys ranged in ages from eight to eighteen, with my young friend being the one and only eight year old. My heart was heavy as he stood there, waiting for them to let him in.

"Hey, Squirt, where have you been? Look at that outfit! Where did you get *that*? What happened to your hair? It looks like you have been to a beauty shop." The cut-downs and negative remarks were mixed with squeals of laughter and mockery. This was almost too difficult for me to bear; I could not imagine how they were making him feel.

Salvador pushed his way through the mob to gain entry to the lobby. It was then that I noticed Luke as he emerged from the side hallway.

"Good evening, Luke. We are back; I just wanted to make sure Salvador was safely returned. We did barely make it by 9:00, didn't we? Things went very well, and again, I thank you for the chance to take Salvador to the festival. He did a very nice job." As I reached through the crowd to return the medicine bag and the paperwork, I saw a small grin on Luke's face—one that said, "I can't believe you don't have a horror story to tell."

"Mission accomplished," I thought. Now, I tried to steal one last glance at my little fellow as I turned to walk back to my car and begin the lonely drive home. I will never forget the look on his face as I managed to wave good-bye. His small hand was gesturing a farewell signal as he stood in the back of the angry mob of "brothers." The look on his face again said, "Take me with you."

"I will see you in the morning, Salvador; good-night." I knew I had to hurry and get out of there, as the emotions were beginning to totally overwhelm me.

The drive back through the country that evening was one of tears, reflection, prayer, and—yes—questions. Who was this kid? Where were his parents? Why did no one seem to want him? Did no one ever see the talent and sweet heart that he had? Isn't love strong enough to break all barriers? And then the toughest question of all: what am I to do next?

It was getting late and dark as I slowly drove up the short driveway leading to our home in the quiet east Texas neighborhood. Tim had not returned home yet from his meetings with the youth staff at our church. "Good," I thought. "This gives me enough time to collect myself and my thoughts before he arrives. I know he will have questions about the night, and I want to be able to answer them without all the emotions."

Before I knew it, time had flown by, and Tim returned from his meetings, anxious about the evening. I gave him all the details, making sure to inform him of the many queries our young friend had fired at me on the return trip to the boys' home. For the next twenty minutes, I simply relived the night, savoring each moment with proud recollection. We could not have planned a more beautiful fairy-tale night. With a delighted sigh and a heavy heart, I finished with the painful moments of the long ride home. "He really did want to stay with me," I informed Tim. "It was a difficult ending to a wonderful evening."

"We surely do have much to pray about, don't we?" he responded as we quietly got ready for bed.

"Yes, I can only hope he is in a good mood tomorrow, and ready to do his work. The school year is flying by, and we have many things to cover before the end of second grade. Hopefully, this positive experience has given him a desire to work hard and prove what he can do in the classroom as well."

"Well, Honey, I know you really love this little guy, and I can see why. He is smart, talented, and does need a home. Let's make this a serious matter of prayer. It just may be that we can get him for a few visits this summer and explore our possibilities. He seems like he would respond well to a loving and supportive home. I had fun with him this evening, if only for that short time. He seemed to like me too, don't you think?"

"Yes. He mentioned that he wished you would have been able to come along to the program with us. I am sure he likes you, too. Who wouldn't?"

With those words, we fell asleep, not really understanding all that was about to transpire in this new venture of ours.

Chapter Eleven:

Fishing Fun

Spring in Texas conjures up the idea of outdoor barbeques, fishing, camping, and hikes at the state park. The pretty rolling hills of east Texas and the numerous fishing lakes and parks are the perfect setting for an energetic boy of eight. Since my husband and I were lovers of nature and the out of doors, we had grandiose plans for getting Salvador for some visits. Wow, what fun we could have on the lake—reeling in some bass and cooking burgers on the grill. With my head full of plans and dreams, I mustered up the courage to make a phone call to the home. This time, it was to ask permission to take Salvador for a Saturday's visit, just to go fishing and spend the day together. My husband had agreed wholeheartedly, so I was ready. This time, I knew we would gain favor and be allowed to take him. After all, by this time in the school year, my name had come up quite a few times as Salvador spoke of me rather favorably to the counselors and the directors at the home. Since we would only be asking for a day's visit, I was very enthusiastic about the possibility, and positive that the request would be granted. This was something Tim and I were praying about, as we did not want to make a wrong move at this juncture.

The next week in school was a busy one—getting all the end-of-the-year testing and the curriculum completed. These students with lower reading abilities had certainly come a long way. I was very proud of them, and very appreciative to Mrs. Wilmarth, who had worked so diligently with me to accomplish our goals. Even though Salvador did not have a reading challenge, he had shown improvement with this work ethic and had made strides with his self-control as well. It had taken a while, but I could actually say that on most days, I was glad that I had kept him. Now, if we could only get permission to have him for a visit on one of these beautiful Saturdays—just for one day.

It was on a very warm and pleasant Monday when I decided to make the call to East Texas Boys Home, asking permission for this fun day. Tim and I had talked, devised a plan, and prayed about every detail of the visit. We would go to the lake for a cookout, grill burgers, and teach young Salvador the art of catching fish. I was quite sure that he had never experienced such a day as we had planned, and I was confident that Mr. Greely could trust us enough to grant the request. Once again, I was thankful for Mrs. Wilmarth. She was able to take the other students to lunch as I made my way to the school office. Memories of just a few weeks ago flashed through my mind, as I dialed that very familiar number.

"Good afternoon, could I please speak with Mr. Greely? This is Mrs. Bost, from Whitehouse Elementary."

In what seemed like an hour, that familiar voice responded. I was shaking inside as I made my appeal to him, again asking for permission to spend a day with my special little friend. I gave the details and made the promises. It seemed like only yesterday that I was doing this very same thing. I felt more confident this time, and ready to hear the answer I wanted.

Perseverance and a fighting spirit surely do pay off. A myriad of happy emotions welled up inside of me as I heard the young director's words: "Yes, Mrs. Bost, we don't see a problem with you and your husband taking Salvador for a day's visit. It is required that you first fill out the paperwork and promise that you will take full responsibility for him. What date did you have in mind?"

At first, I could not believe that I was hearing these words. "We are really making progress," I thought. "We would like to take him fishing this Saturday. Having him back by 9:00 PM as before should pose no problem at all."

"Ok, Mrs. Bost. I believe you and your husband understand our process now, so we will authorize this visit."

"Oh, Mr. Greely, thank you so very much. I am pleased to hear that you will allow us this opportunity. We would like to pick him up around 8:00 AM on Saturday. We have a fun-filled day planned, which includes a visit to Tyler State Park for fishing and barbequing. I know that he will be excited to go with us, and I am so appreciative for the chance. When do we meet to take care of the paperwork?"

"Just drop by tomorrow after school, and we can discuss all the 'particulars. I will have the forms ready, with a copy of what is required of you and your husband as the caretakers of this young man. It is certainly not an easy thing you are asking, but we here at the home can only hope that this visit will help Salvador. You have my best wishes. I will see you at 4:00 PM tomorrow."

Wow! It wasn't as difficult as I had first imagined. We were really getting Salvador. He would be spending the day with us. It did take a few minutes for the good news to actually sink in. I immediately dialed my husband's number to share the unbelievable news. Of course, he was elated and very surprised that things had turned out so well. We could continue working on the detailed plans for this fun-filled day.

I was able to keep the good news from Salvador for a few days, certain that it would be best to wait until a closer time to let him in on our plans. I was able to do just that until the day before.

Finishing up the assignments on that long Friday, I waited patiently for the right moment to approach Salvador about the next day's plan. It was time for the students to pack their belongings for dismissal when I decided to speak with him.

"Hey, Salvador, do not forget your math workbook and your reading book. Remember, you do have a few things to finish up this weekend," I reminded him.

"Yeah, I guess I will have time to do that; there is not much else going on around that place."

"Wait a minute. Would you like to go fishing tomorrow with Tim and me? Do you like hamburgers on the grill? What do you think about spending the day with us?"

"Are you kidding? That would be great! Did you talk to Mr. Greely again? Did he say I could? Yes, yes, yes! I would love that."

By this time in our relationship, Salvador really knew that Tim and I genuinely cared for him. There was proof that what had seemed like impossibilities had been made possibilities, so he did display a more positive and believing attitude. An expectant, happy smile appeared on that beautiful face, and once again, he showed signs of real love and happiness. This was truly a moment to cherish.

Watching him skip to the bus was a moment that I wished could have been frozen in time. He was a carefree eight year old who finally had a reason to skip, a reason to be elated about a Friday afternoon and the upcoming weekend. Words could not express my joy.

That evening found Tim and me excitedly rushing off to the grocery store for all the food items and snacks that we would need for the big day, not to mention the fishing supplies and other necessary items. We had several rods and reels; they just needed a little repair work. Since we enjoyed camping, and were youth pastors, there was no challenge in putting together our day's necessities for a once in a lifetime day with Salvador.

"We need to wrap this up, Honey, and get some rest," Tim wearily announced at about 11:00 PM. "We have a very big day tomorrow, and we need our rest too. I wonder if Salvador is as excited as we are. If so, I guess he may not be sleeping much tonight either. I do think we have thought of everything, so let's call it a day and get to sleep." With that, I double-checked the food list, and agreed with him that we had it all covered.

"OK, good night, Sweetheart. Sleep well. Just make sure the clock is set for 7:00 AM. We are to pick him up by 9:00, and I do not want to be late. We want to make the most of this day, and cherish each moment. Sleep well."

"Good night. I will see you bright and early in the morning." With that, the lamp was clicked off, and I was left to dream of a perfect day with a perfect boy in a perfect setting.

In what seemed like a few short hours, the East Texas sun peered into our bedroom window, announcing the dawn of a brand new day, filled with new adventures and lots of fun.

"Hey, it is almost 7:00, and the clock will sound any minute now. Let's get up and get this day started," I happily said as I shook my sleepy husband. "Wake up. We only have to load the day's supplies and pick up Salvador. I am sure he will be waiting."

After double-checking our food and supply list, we were finally on our way to East Texas Boys Home to pick up our little man. Tim and I chatted nervously about the day and just how we wanted things to be for Salvador. This was another of those God-ordained times that was in the master plan way back in October. I again whispered a prayer of thanksgiving to my

Heavenly Father for dealing with me the way He did on that fall day when Mrs. Mason brought this troubled boy to my classroom. My, I was amazed at just how situations can change just in the course of a few months.

It was a few minutes before 9:00 AM when we pulled into the winding, tree-lined drive leading up to the main building of the home. Salvador's dormitory was just to the right of this building. My heart was beating like an eight-year-old kid on Christmas morning. As Tim stopped the truck at the entrance, I saw a little face peering out from the blinds in the lobby. Yes! I guess he must have been waiting on us with anticipation.

As we completed the paperwork, and were given the medicines for the day, Salvador proudly pranced up and down the hallway. I can still remember what he wore that day: his faded jeans, and the dark blue tee-shirt that we had given him a few weeks back. He was truly happy and ready.

The ride out to the lake was filled with laughs, jokes, and plans for catching "the big one." It only seemed like a few short minutes when I announced: "Hey, I can see the water; we are almost there."

Salvador's curious gaze was worth all the time and effort we had put into making this day happen. The excitement was contagious, and my inner child was exploding within me as well. Times like these always reminded me of my own childhood, where fishing was a normal activity for my dad and me. In fact, I was privileged to go on my first fishing trip as an infant. My young father wrapped me in a blanket and placed me in that aluminum row boat and away we went on the water. What a contrast of timing for a lively and energetic young boy!

Ah, Lake Tyler in the springtime! What a beautiful sight to see! The glistening blue water, the stately pine trees, and yes—the fishing barge! This was the place to be on a warm Saturday in Tyler, especially for an eight-year-old boy who had never been fishing before.

"This is it; this is it, Salvador!" I yelled as we all emerged from the loaded truck. "Grab the rods and the tackle boxes; I will get the picnic basket. Hopefully, we will have a few nice ones to go in the bucket before lunch." With that, we scampered down to the water's edge, and found a nice place to set up for the day.

"How do we do this?" Salvador asked, as he attempted baiting the hook. It was so much fun to watch his inquisitive face as this new experience was unfolding before him. It did not take long for him to grab the minnow and slowly, but cautiously place the slimy little creature on the hook. After waiting just a few minutes, the cork went under. "Reel it in!" Tim yelled. "You have one on the line!" I could not resist that familiar line that my dad and grandpa used to yell when I was fishing with them as a child: "Bending rods and smiling faces!" they would scream, as a happy little girl wound and wound until her hand felt numb.

Let's go fishing!

"You have him, Salvador, you have him!"

As Tim ran over to show him how to take the glistening bass off the hook, I stood back and captured another priceless moment with this bundle of energy. His smile was one of sheer bliss and total happiness.

After a few nice bass were in the bucket, it was time to take a break and enjoy the delicious lunch we had packed. The three of us sat down, chatted about the big "catch of the day," and gobbled up the sandwiches and chips we had packed. This was again a time to remember.

Time is a precious commodity; sometimes it seems to fly by, and at other times it seems to stand still. For this one teacher, and this one little boy, these moments certainly seemed to fly by.

Chapter Twelve:

Tough Love

Spring fever had surely hit our second-grade classroom as the students stared out the windows to see the bright blue Texas skies. Their hearts yearned for the playground, soccer fields, and black-top pavement. Jump ropes and kick balls replaced brushes, pencils, and writing tablets in the young minds of my small family. One may define "difficult" as the ability to control and teach thirteen curious and active young minds during the last eight weeks of school. But, being a young and active educator, I took the challenge seriously to provide a successful end to what could have been a disastrous school year—at least from that fateful day back in October when Salvador Garcia entered our world.

It was on one of those warm beautiful days in early May that Salvador bounded into the room wearing that cute little outfit from his memorable evening on stage. Surprisingly, the pants and shirt still appeared brand new, with only a few rough marks on the white canvas shoes. The suspenders fit snugly around his little chest, and he wore a smile of confidence, coupled with an air of expectancy. It was going to be a good day, for sure—or, at least, it started out that way.

As the day progressed, I realized that I needed to get one last reading assessment completed for the end-of-the-year folders.

"Class, we will only have about ten questions to complete, and then we will go outdoors to play." As I handed out the sheets to the eager students, Salvador only gazed at me. I had seen that look too many times before. It said, "You can't make me; I do not want to."

"OK, class, you will need to read each question, and write a short answer to complete each thought. I know you can do this. We have worked hard on this all year."

"I will *not* do this stupid work!" bellowed Salvador. "I don't care about this work. I want to go outside!"

"You will be able to go out when you finish," I firmly responded. "Oh no," I thought. "Lord, has all my work thus far been in vain? What about the love, clothes, school supplies, and even the trip to the lake? Has all this so soon been forgotten?"

As I calmly and patiently instructed him to complete the work, he proceeded to break the pencils I had bought for him, and as he angrily threw the broken stubs across the floor, I moved to the side with a look of disgust and hopelessness on my face.

"Salvador, you will not be able to play soccer when we go outside this afternoon. You will sit out and finish your work."

"I don't care," was his belligerent response. At that moment, I sincerely felt that all the successes from days gone by had been tossed to the wind.

As the students finished, we proceeded with the morning's work and slowly watched the clock until lunch.

At last, afternoon recess! It could have not come soon enough for these little balls of energy. As we gathered the playground supplies and soccer balls, the students made an orderly line to exit the building. Salvador chatted excitedly with his soccer pal, Wiley. They almost always dominated the soccer game, and Salvador showed tremendous skill with his feet. Oh how he loved the game.

"OK, boys and girls, let's move outside now." Salvador seemed to have forgotten his morning's choice to bypass the reading assessment. He was smiling, jumping around, and preparing for the big game.

As we entered the playground area, I calmly and lovingly reminded him that he had to sit our during today's recess. "Remember your choice not to do the assessment this morning, Salvador? You will not be allowed to play soccer today. Stay here and finish your work."

That energetic and happy face quickly turned to anger and fits of unhappiness. He stomped off to the side of the building and crouched down near the outside water fountain. It was at this spot that Salvador commenced to sit and sulk—or this is what I *thought* he was going to do.

I left him to turn my attention to the others who, by now, had spread out across the various areas of the massive playground.

"Come shoot baskets with me, Mrs. Bost," said Wiley. Since Salvador was not free to play soccer, Wiley turned his attention to the asphalt-topped basketball court.

"Great, Wiley, I will shoot with you." These words only served to fuel more anger from the disgruntled Salvador.

As Wiley and I began our game of H-O-R-S-E, I could see from the corner of my eye a very distracted and mad little boy.

"Good shot, Mrs. Bost!" yelled Wiley, as I dropped a ten-foot jumper from the corner of the court. "Let's see if I can make that one." We were engaged in our fun game, only to be interrupted by three blood-curdling squeals from the girls who had been jumping rope near the building.

"Mrs. Bost, Mrs. Bost!" came their desperate and startled cries. "Look at Salvador! He is messing up your clothes—the ones you bought for him. Stop him! Stop him!"

I quickly glanced up to the spot by the water fountain, only to see a mud-covered boy, furiously throwing handfuls of red wet soil on that pretty white shirt, aqua-colored pants, and yes, even the neat white shoes that he had danced so skillfully in only two weeks earlier.

"Oh no, I thought. What is he doing now?" Understanding that he was jealous of the time I was spending with Wiley, I chose to avoid him, allowing him the opportunity to process his emotions without intrusion or frustration.

"Those are not *my* clothes; they are *his*," I responded to the upset girls. "If he wants to ruin them, that is *his* choice. I gave them to him."

Showing signs of misunderstanding and questions, the girls returned to their jump ropes, while Wiley and I finished our game of "H-O-R-S-E."

It was difficult for me to laugh and play when inside, my heart was breaking. True love is really unconditional, and must always pass the test of adversity. This was another one of the tests that I had to pass.

"Line up, boys and girls. It is time to go inside. Salvador, please brush the dirt off your pants and shoes. I do not want to mess up the new carpet in my classroom."

As the students gathered the equipment and prepared to go inside, all eyes were on that dirty, mud-covered little soccer player, who had transformed himself from a talented dancer to a hate-filled filthy second grader. My, what a change.

The remainder of that afternoon seemed uneventful as we completed our math and science stations. Salvador was a mess, but yet appeared thoughtful and reflective as the dismissal bell drew near. Finally, another difficult day had come to an end.

"Good-bye, Candy. I will see you in the morning. Good-bye, Wiley, thanks for a fun game of basketball. Don't forget your reading homework, Travis."

As Salvador approached the door for my usual good-bye hug, he quickly pulled away and made a disgusted scowl in my direction.

"Bye, Salvador. I love you. I will see you tomorrow. Remember, I love you."

Chapter Thirteen:

Love Note

Returning to the classroom the next spring morning was not as pleasant as it should have been for this teacher. The memory of that cute outfit covered in mud and dirt almost brought the previous day to life again. What a nightmare.

As the students gathered their materials for the morning's work, my eyes fell upon Salvador at his cubby. Wearing wrinkled jeans, a pair of scuffed-up old shoes, and that faded striped shirt from his first day back in October, he angrily tossed his reader on the table. I knew it was going to be one of those days.

We got through the morning schedule without a major incident, and then soon, it was time for lunch. I really believe those perceptive eight year olds could feel my pain from the day before. It was almost as if they had a new respect and love for me, sensing my pain.

At lunch, Salvador talked quietly and calmly with Wiley. Maybe he felt bad about his antics from the playground. Maybe he did have regrets. It was sad to see such a hardened little heart at the tender age of eight. Even through the pain, my love for him seemed to increase, in spite of the hurt he had caused me. "That is unconditional love," God reminded me. "Keep going. Keep showing Me to him."

When dismissal finally came, the students lined up to board the buses. We were slowly but surely completing another school year. Ahh! Summer is just around the corner, I kept reminding myself. I would certainly miss these little ones, and sometimes the thought of Salvador's future would interrupt my sweet images of summer break. "What would happen to him? Oh, I will be able to follow his progress in third grade. I could have lunch with him, and stay in touch with his new teacher. All will be fine; all will be fine," I told myself as I returned from the bus-loading area to clean my room for the day. A room filled with activities of a hard day's work can be quite untidy and cluttered by day's end.

Rushing to straighten the room and get to my paperwork, I noticed a crumpled sheet of lined paper on my desk that had not been there when the day ended. "What could that be?" I pondered. Usually, I would have just tossed it into the waste basket, but something about this sheet of paper said, "Read me. Open me." I could not resist. Unfolding the small sheet of dirty, smudged paper, I saw scribbled in a second-grade hand:

> Dear Mrs Bost
> I am sorry about the clothes do you still love me?
>
> Love
> Sal your pal ♥

Gazing at that small sheet of paper through tear-filled eyes, the realization came to me that his heart was softening. He felt bad about what he had done. He was sorry. He knew he had hurt me, and he was sorry for his actions. Such a feeling of success and fulfillment flooded my heart. But then I realized that, in his understanding of love, he thought my love stopped when he disappointed me. He had never experienced true unconditional love, so now he had to know that I really did still love him. I could hardly wait for the next day to talk to him, hug him, and assure him that I still loved him. That night, I fell asleep with a beautiful thought of a new day filled with love and forgiveness.

The next morning dawned with a freshness and newness that was exciting. Spring was in the air, and each new flower in bud seemed to lift its head to the warm sun, awaiting full opening.

"Good morning, boys and girls," I cheerily said before our work day began. Of course, my eyes fell longingly and lovingly to my Salvador. What was on his mind? Had the instability and hate of a night at the boys' home cause him to forget the note? Was his heart still moldable?

Once the students were busy with their morning seatwork, I sweetly called Salvador to my desk. He approached with caution, I believe, still feeling so bad about the clothes he had ruined. Holding the crumpled note in my hand, I said, "Salvador, I got your note on my desk yesterday. I thank you for writing it, and I want you to know that I still do love you. I will always love you. Remember what I told you the first day I met you? I do love you, Salvador, and nothing can change that. I forgive you, and I am not mad at you."

His big brown eyes seemed to lighten up, as he gazed up from his cold stare at the floor. It was as if he wanted to believe me, but just could not bring himself to do it. He had never in his short life been loved *in spite of* what he had done wrong. This was almost too much for him to take in, but somehow I believed he trusted me, and that he did believe me.

"Do you still have the clothes, Salvador? Do you like them? Do you want to wear them again?"

"Yes, yes!" was his immediate response. "I do like them, and I do want to wear them again, but they are ruined. They are very dirty."

"Where are they, Salvador? Do you still have them?

"They are in a brown paper bag under my bed at the home," he said. "I didn't want Luke and the other counselors to know what I had done, so I hid them under my bed. I didn't want to throw them away, so I put them there."

"OK, Salvador, listen to me. If you still want to wear them, just bring them to me tomorrow. I will take them home and wash them. I will try to get all the mud and the dirt out. What about the shoes?"

"The shoes are in the bag too. I just knew the counselors would be mad and be mean to me if they knew exactly what had happened."

"Just bring the bag to me, Salvador, and I will try to scrub the stains out and make it all better so you can wear that outfit again. You looked so nice in it. I will soak the clothes and scrub the shoes. I believe you will be able to wear the entire outfit again soon."

"Thank you, Mrs. Bost," came his muffled and quiet response.

"He is getting it," I thought. "Maybe there is still hope."

Just seeing a light in his eyes and hearing the emotion in his words again gave me that much-needed encouragement to tackle yet another day. It is true: love is a choice, but it also involves action. His frustration and hate seemed to melt away in the hope that his clothes were wearable again, and that I still loved him. I only hoped I would not disappoint him.

Washing, soaking, and scrubbing Texas mud out of a white-and-blue outfit at times seemed impossible, but with each stroke of the brush, I felt a deep and new love for this little boy. Each wash cycle seemed to demonstrate the cleansing of his heart. The stains seemed to disappear, and the brightness of the fabric once again appeared like new.

Washing his shirt and pants reminded me that our lives are all stained, dirty, and appear ugly at times, but they are never to be thrown away or abandoned. I again realized that unconditional love does not think of itself, but of others. "And now these three remain: faith, hope, and love. But the greatest of these is love" (I Corinthians 13:13).

Chapter Fourteen:

Clean Treasures

Finally, the day came to take that cherished outfit back to the little boy for whom it was so lovingly purchased. I had neatly placed the pants and shirt on hangers and put the shoes in a small box, hoping they would be as desirable as the day we shopped for them in the mall. The excitement I felt that spring morning in May brought tears of joy to my eyes. With deep satisfaction and a bit of anticipation, I arrived to my classroom earlier than usual to hide the treasures until the proper time of unveiling.

The morning's agenda began as usual with no complications or distractions. The students were delighted about the approaching summer break, and I must admit that I was, too. The progress they had made in reading was commendable, and I knew the test scores would prove it. This certainly had been a year to remember. When the day finally ended, I beckoned Salvador to my desk for the revealing of the "new" outfit. Maybe he had forgotten that I had promised him I would do my best to restore the clothes. Maybe he hadn't hoped for much, as his life had been full of shattered dreams and broken promises.

Pulling the box out from behind my desk, I noticed a flicker of light in his curious brown eyes. The hangers were in the coat closet, and I retrieved them with the excitement of a child on Christmas morning.

"What do you think of this, Salvador? I gave it my best, and most of the stains did come out. I am sorry it took so long, but . . . well . . . here are your 'new' clothes."

The astonished look of his little tanned face was worth every wash cycle and every sacrifice I had made to create this moment.

"Thank you, Mrs. Bost, thank you. I figured I would never see this outfit again . . . ever! I really messed it up, didn't I? But it looks good now. Thank you!"

"You are welcome, Salvador. I love you, and you are worth it. Always remember that I love you, and I always will. "

He then happily skipped out to the bus line, gripping tightly the box and holding the hangers in his small fingers. "Love is a powerful force and it often demands action," I thought, as I watched him board the bus for home.

With only about two weeks of school left, the students and I were busy, completing assessments, creating stories, and yes—reading. What I had thought would become a disaster back in October had actually become a positive experience. This Salvador Garcia had become a part of our little family, and the students had loved him and accepted him as one of their own. Even though the journey for me had been challenging, I had to admit, it had been worth it. This unlovable, unwanted student had found a home of sorts in our classroom, and we now could not imagine the school year without him. With a thankful heart, and a deep breath of satisfaction, I packed my things to head home, savoring the thoughts of another wonderful and memorable day.

Chapter Fifteen:

Say the Words

My husband Tim and I had also relished our own experiences with Salvador. As youth pastors, we had been able to take him with us to youth events and church activities. That day at Lake Tyler was forever etched in our minds, and Sundays after church when we took him to lunch with us were very special. The thought of adoption had crossed our minds occasionally, but we knew that would need to be a serious matter of prayer and wise counsel; however, it was not out of the question. We certainly did not want to mention anything to Salvador, knowing that another disappointment in his life would not be good for him, or for us, so we kept the matter to ourselves, and only pondered it from time to time.

At last—the final day of school. With mixed emotions, I prepared myself for tears and a little sadness. Life without these thirteen second-graders seemed dismal, but I also realized after a couple of lazy summer months, the desire for a brand new group of eager learners would burn within.

Paperwork duties are always tedious at the end of an academic school year, and along with that, test scores and assessments have to be done to satisfy state requirements. On this day, I simply needed one more short reading assessment to place in student files for their upcoming third grade year. With Salvador's excellent reading ability, I was confident that he would score at the top of the class. Each student had made tremendous strides, but Salvador had come to me as a strong reader, and for this, I was grateful. At least that had not been my focus for him. As I walked from table to table distributing the small test forms, the angry troubled look on Salvador's face again said, "You can't make me!"

"Oh, my," I thought. "This is the last day of school. I can't go backward. We have accomplished so much, and since he was sporting that "new" outfit today, I just knew he would cooperate with a thankful heart for all I had done for him.

"I don't want to do that work!" he exploded, throwing the new pencil I had sharpened for him across the room. "I am tired of all this work, and it is the last day of school. I want to go outside and play one last game of soccer. I *hate* all this stupid work!"

"Mrs. Wilmarth, will you please take the students outside to play while I speak privately with Salvador?"

"Yes, of course," came Mrs. Wilmarth's startled and cooperative reply.

The other boys and girls had grown accustomed to similar outbursts, but no one was thinking *this* would happen on the last day. I guess we all thought we had gotten past this point. I, for one, was weary of these episodes, and I really didn't feel as if I had any love or patience left to deal with this young man.

Once the others had exited the room, I trudged across the room, only to find a mad and frustrated student staring at the small desk before him, eyes ablaze with anger toward me and the whole world.

"I told you I didn't want to do that test, and I still don't! I hate you, and I hate these clothes too!" With that, he jerked the almost white shoes from his feet, and hurled them across the room. As they bounced off the cement block wall, I knew I had had enough. All patience and love seemed to have been erased.

Retrieving the shoes that once held the small feet of a great dancer, I marched across to where he sat, put him into the nearest chair and declared with authority—"*Put these shoes on your feet; they belong to you. They are your shoes. I bought them for you. They are not mine; they are yours. Now put them on!*"

Salvador had never once heard this voice from me. I had always spoken soft but stern words to him. Even when I disciplined him before, I spoke firmly, yet gently. He was startled beyond belief at my response. With hesitation, and a little fear, he placed the shoes back on his feet. He knew I meant business.

Then, in another fit of anger, he again reminded me that he hated me, and that he didn't even like those ugly clothes.

"I hate you! I never wanted to go to your house! Riding in your car was not fun either. I hate you! I don't even like these stupid clothes!"

Fiery darts of hurt and anger seemed to roll off his tongue like rushing water over a cliff.

"Well, excuse me," I retorted. "I *thought* you wanted to go in my car to the mall that day. I *thought* you enjoyed going to my house. You surely acted like you had fun. I am so sorry. I will never make you ride in my car again. I will not force you to visit our house again! Please forgive me! I thought you wanted that. I am so sorry for making you do what you did not want to do. It won't happen again!"

Then, those big, angry eyes softened, and a change came over him that altered everything. Hot tears of pain began to stream down his face and he fell into my arms crying out, "But I do love you. I just do not know what to do. You are the only one who has even loved me." His little body trembled and shook as he poured out the truth in sobs.

"It is the last day of school. I am so afraid. What will I do next? I will never see you again, and I am scared."

As he held tightly to me, arms around my waist, his small body shook almost uncontrollably. I held him tightly, tears falling from my own eyes.

"Oh, Salvador, I love you so much. I told you that I would always love you, and that nothing could ever change that. It is *not* over. Since school is finished, we will spend more time together. We plan to take more fishing trips, and even take a camping trip to the lake. I will have more time, and even next year, I will come have lunch with you at school, and help with your homework. It is *not* over, Sweetheart."

We both spent several quiet moments, allowing the healing warmth of love and acceptance to flow over us, and the tears to wash away the insecurities and misunderstandings of days gone by.

Pulling him away from me to gaze into his bright eyes, I assured him again of my love and support.

"It is all OK, Salvador. I love you."

"I love you too, Mrs. Bost."

Those words were as sweet as the honey of a thousand bees, and those once bitter eyes now seemed to pierce my heart with the tenderness and innocence of the loving child that stood before me. What a moment!

When the others returned from their surprise recess time, they didn't quite grasp the fact that they had a brand-new classmate and a renewed teacher. The remainder of that last school day was almost a blur, but I do know that it was very emotional, and filled with lots of love, tearful good-byes, and tender moments as this small family parted ways for the sweet days of summer.

Chapter Sixteen:

Summer Surprise

Summer for a teacher is a wonderful time of refreshing and renewal, a time to trade the rigorous schedules and paper grading to relaxing days with family and friends. This summer would hold special and unique times with my husband and our new little friend, Salvador Who knew? Just maybe the process of adoption would take shape, and we could spend even more memorable days together.

It was during that summer that the director of the home trusted us even more with Salvador, so we were able to take him to church with us often. Our love for Salvador spread to the other boys in the home. Since we were youth pastors, the teen-age boys were allowed to visit the youth group, and some even played on the church basketball team. We had become known as friends of the home, but more affectionately as Salvador's "parents." All of the older boys knew about our special bond, and most approved. These were happy times, as we continued to pray about our future with this changed little boy.

It was on one of those beautiful summer evenings that a phone call came from East Texas Boys Home that would put a very different perspective on our plans for a family of three. My husband, Tim, was outdoors on the patio grilling some burgers, while I was inside, preparing the other dishes. The ringing of the kitchen wall phone interrupted my work, and silenced my thoughts.

"Hello," I said, expecting a familiar voice of a long-distance call from family in North Carolina.

"Hi, Mrs. Bost . . . c-c-can you come h-h-here? I d-d-don't know what to do. The home is cl-cl-cl-closing. Salvador h-h-has gone! I will b-b-b-be leaving later t-t-today. I am scared!" I recognized the voice as that of Amigo—at least that is what we all called him—a thirteen-year-old Hispanic kid who had been a part of the basketball team at the church. Amigo's broken English and troubled cries for help were upsetting, to say the least.

"Slow down, Amigo. What are you talking about? Salvador is gone? Gone where? You must be mistaken. We just saw Salvador a few days ago, and he seemed to be fine. This cannot be true. Now, tell me again what you are talking about."

In his serious and hurting voice, young Amigo repeated his message as best as he could.

"No, I thought. *"No!"* Stunned, and broken, I burst open the door leading to the patio to summon Tim.

"What in the world is wrong?" Tim questioned, looking up from the grill. He knew, by the look on my face, that something terrible must have transpired in the few minutes since he left the kitchen to put the burgers on the grill.

By this time, the shock and pain from Amigo's words had settled in my head, and all I could picture was a little lost boy who had been rejected *again* and sent away. Where was he? Was Amigo right? Who had closed the home? Why? These and a thousand other questions buzzed in my mind. I know Amigo had asked for us to come, but the very thought of seeing Salvador's empty bed, and his vacated room were too much for me to bear.

"Honey, I will go check it out. You stay here and pray. There must have been a terrible mistake. Maybe this is a joke."

Somehow, inside, I knew it wasn't. I had heard the fear in Amigo's voice. It was real.

The next forty-five minutes seemed more like an entire day, and when I spotted that red Silverado truck pull in the drive, a feeling of temporary relief settled over me. Maybe he will have a good report; maybe this *has* all been a dream.

As Tim climbed from the truck, I noticed his gait was slow and reflective. The usual happy and carefree grin on his face was lost amidst the serious and stoic look.

"What is happening out there, Tim? Do you have good news? Is Salvador truly gone? Tell me that Amigo's words are not true."

With the tenderness and patience not found by many, my husband held me closely and confirmed the report.

"Yes, Honey, the home has been closed. There were reports of abuse from the counselors and workers. The state authorities were called in to investigate the findings. They were found guilty. The boys have been placed in various centers and foster homes around the state."

"But where is our Salvador? Could they not tell you? What did they do with him?" I cried. This was the news I was not totally prepared to hear.

The next few days were spent trying to sort through feelings of hurt, anger, and frustration. Due to the sensitive matter of the accusations and the state's involvement, all the cases were kept confidential. No one was allowed to ask questions, and absolutely no information was given, under any circumstance. No phone calls were returned, and there was no one to appeal to. It was during these times that questions flooded our minds, and the memories of precious moments gone by were held tightly. In the lonely hours, God drew us close and confirmed His love to us. We had not made a mistake in loving this little boy and demonstrating unconditional love for him. Our strong faith in God sustained us in the dark hours of sadness. "His ways are higher than our ways." God's Word spoke and comforted us. His Word remained true and authoritative. I rested in the fact that I had been obedient to God's plan for our journey from the beginning, although I was hesitant at first. Surely, all was not lost. One small lost, unlovable little boy, so filled with hate, had come to experience real love for the first time in his life. I cherished this truth, and every precious memory we had made together. Maybe all was *not* lost!

Chapter Seventeen:

Real Mom

As the lazy days of summer seemed to slowly pass, my thoughts often turned to young Salvador. Our attempts to get any information about his whereabouts failed.

"God, please help me to know he is OK," I prayed. "Give me some indication that he is being cared for, and that he is in the hands of a loving family who will continue to build on the foundation of love that was started."

That prayer was answered on a beautiful day late in August as I was shopping at our local mall for back-to-school deals.

"Hello, Mrs. Bost," came a friendly and familiar voice. Turning quickly, I soon recognized the face of Renaldo, one of the older boys who had lived in the home. Overjoyed to see one of our boys, I reached to give him a hug.

"Renaldo, it is go wonderful to see you. How in the world have you been? Where are you living now?"

"Oh, when I turned eighteen, I had to find a place of my own, so I came back to Tyler to live with my uncle. I have a job here, and I plan to start college in just a few weeks."

"That is such good news. I am very proud of you. I always knew you would find your way, Renaldo. Keep up the good work."

Before I had much time to relish his accomplishments, the words gushed out, "Have you heard from Salvador? Do you know what happened to him? Where did he get placed? Do you know? Tell me, please!"

"Yes, Mrs. Bost, I was hoping I would see you sometime to tell you the news. Our group home was attending a rodeo in Houston just last month. I was in line to get my popcorn and drink, when I spotted another group of boys in line next to our line. Salvador noticed me, and he rushed over to say hello. We talked, and he seemed happy, telling me that he now lives with a Christian family in the Houston area. He was doing well, and was nicely dressed. You would have been proud of him, Mrs. Bost. We did not talk much about our problems at the home, but he did say one thing you may be glad to hear."

"What was it, Renaldo? Did he mention Tim and me? Did he say he would like to come back to Tyler?"

"No, but he did say that he liked his new home, his new family and his new mother, but that his *real* mom lived in Tyler. I think he must have meant you, Mrs. Bost. Do you think so?"

"Uh... What? E-e-excuse me, Renaldo, "I stuttered, hot tears forming in my eyes. "I must go."

Chapter Eighteen:

And Love Remains

At the date of this writing, it has been twenty-seven years since I last saw Salvador Garcia. That night at the Spring Music Festival almost seems like yesterday... a happy teacher holding the hand of the new boy tightly as both enjoyed his debut on stage. Then, at times, that night seems like fifty years ago, a lost memory in the halls of time. I have often visualized our lives with him, and I have asked thousands of questions about purpose, faith, destiny, and yes, even prayer.

Today, God's presence surrounds me, and I rest in the assurance that "in all things God works for the good of those who love Him, who have been called according to His purpose" (Romans 8:28).

There certainly is satisfaction in knowing that, for that time and place, God spoke, I listened, and His purposes prevailed. Just maybe I don't need to know everything. Maybe the pain of knowing the whole story is being shielded from me by the same loving Heavenly Father that I introduced Salvador Garcia to in those months in 1987–1988.

So, is this really an unfinished love story, or is it finished? I will leave that for you, the reader, to decide. For me, on most days, it is finished because I know it is well with me. It is sometimes unfinished on those days when I wonder just what the thirty-five year-old Salvador thinks about love. But, for now, I will cherish those words, "I love you too, Mrs. Bost."

"And now, these three remain: faith, hope, and love. But the greatest of these is love." —I Corinthians 13:13

"Many waters cannot quench love, neither can the floods drown it; if a man would give all the substance of his house for love, it would utterly be condemned." —Song of Solomon 8:7

Dedication

Dedicated to all who feel lost and alone in this big, often cruel world. You are loved!

Salvador Garcia 1988

Acknowledgements

I would like to personally thank and acknowledge the students at First Assembly Christian School (Winston Salem, North Carolina) in the classes from 1992–2012 for listening to this story and believing in its value. I am not sure I would have ever begun the writing process without their encouragement to do so.

Also, I thank the classes at Winston Salem Christian School from 2012–present for being the greatest encouragers and cheerleaders as I walked through the writing stages. On days when I felt like giving up, they offered the fuel for the drive. Thank you, Lions! Particularly, I want to thank Daniel Shegog, who handed me a small publishing house card on September 24, 2015, saying, "Maybe this will encourage you to finish your book, Mrs. Bost." From that day until the last word was typed, this six-year project became an easy one to complete. Thanks, Daniel.

I acknowledge my loving husband, who, for over forty years, has believed in me and always told me I could do anything. Thank you, baby.

To my parents, Paul and Betty Bennick who gave me that early confidence and love to reach deep within to be all I was created to be. Thanks, Mom and Dad.

To my daughter, Laresey, for her love and support, as well as my goddaughters, Endyia, Emani, Harmeni, and Diamond. Thank you all.

To my spiritual mentors, Bishop James C. and Joyce Hash, who, for over twenty-five years, taught me about a God of faith, love, and impossibilities. Thanks, Bishop and Ma.

MOST IMPORTANTLY, to my Heavenly Father, Who is above everyone and everything. He gave me Salvador for a season to love and to teach. Without Him, there would be no story to tell, and no book to pen. He daily pours His love out on me, allowing me to love the unlovable and model these lessons to my students. He is, and always will be love!

About the Author

Carol Bost has been involved in education for thirty-six years, teaching in Tennessee, Texas, and North Carolina. Her experience has included the public and the private sectors, reaching students from kindergarten through eighth grades.

After her transformation to Christ in high school, Carol immediately began seeking God's divine will and purpose for her life. Graduating from Lee College in 1979, Carol taught in the Bradley County School System where she was named "Outstanding Young Educator" by the district. She also taught in the Polk County School System before moving to Texas, teaching in both the Whitehouse Independent School District and the Tyler Independent School District.

Carol Bost

Being involved in ministry with her husband Tim, Carol then moved home to North Carolina. In 1992, Carol began teaching at First Assembly Christian School, (currently Winston Salem Christian School) where she teaches middle school Bible classes today. In 2007, she was inducted into "The National Honor Roll's List of Outstanding American Teachers."

"God has blessed me with a wide variety of teaching experiences, but none can come close to the experience I had with young Salvador. Getting this message out has been a dream come true."

Carol has been married to her high school sweetheart, Tim Bost, for thirty-seven years, and they reside in the Winston Salem area.

If you would like further information about having Carol speak in your school or church, please contact her at cbostezekiel@att.net.